Dan Sch[...]
11372 N. Sawtooth Rd
Tucson   AZ 85737

(520) 575-0569

Here
We
Stand!

"In the final analysis,
Truth is not a human system
or a rationalist ideology, and
certainly not a private opinion;
rather truth is the person of
Jesus Christ   p 94 Veith

The Alliance of Confessing Evangelicals, formed in 1994, is an association of evangelical pastors, teachers, and leaders of parachurch organizations. The association's goal is the recovery of the biblical, apostolic witness by the evangelical movement. *Here We Stand!* consists of papers presented at the ACE's summit meeting in Cambridge, Massachusetts, April 17–20, 1996.

Here
We
Stand!

A Call from
Confessing Evangelicals

Edited by
James Montgomery Boice
and Benjamin E. Sasse

Baker Books
A Division of Baker Book House Co
Grand Rapids, Michigan 49516

©1996 by the Alliance of Confessing Evangelicals

Published by Baker Books
a division of Baker Book House Company
P.O. Box 6287, Grand Rapids, MI 49516-6287

Library of Congress Cataloging-in-Publication Data

  Here we stand : a call from confessing evangelicals / edited by James Montgomery Boice and Benjamin E. Sasse.
     p.   cm.
  Includes bibliographical references and index.
  ISBN 0-8010-1134-5 (cloth)
  1. Reformed Church—Doctrines. 2. Theology, Doctrinal.
  I. Boice, James Montgomery, 1938–   . II. Sasse, Benjamin E.
BX9422.2.H46 1996
230′.046—dc20   96-26128

For information about academic books, resources for Christian leaders, and all new releases available from Baker Book House, visit our web site:
http://www.bakerbooks.com/

To
Robert D. Preus
Defender of the Faith
in memory of his founding role
in the formation of the
Alliance of Confessing Evangelicals

Def. = definition

⊤< joined/union/related

↔ Traveling different roads / directions

* = significant statement

§ = significant quote

Ref. Bible reference

B means reference book

S* something special

⇒ Both Traveling the same direction

What Chapters stand out above ✱

Contents

Preface

James Montgomery Boice

The Cambridge Declaration, which follows this preface, and the eight papers that support it are the products of a historic meeting of 120 evangelical pastors, teachers, and leaders of parachurch organizations that took place in Cambridge, Massachusetts, April 17–20, 1996. Believing that the evangelical movement is in crisis, these persons met to call the evangelical church in America to repent of its worldliness and to seek to recover the biblical, apostolic doctrines that alone empower the church and provide integrity for its witness. The meeting was called by the Alliance of Confessing Evangelicals, whose purpose statement reads:

> The Alliance of Confessing Evangelicals exists to call the church, amidst our dying culture, to repent of its worldliness, to recover and confess the truth of God's Word as did the Reformers, and to see that truth embodied in doctrine, worship and life.

In those four days of meetings papers were presented on four subjects: "Our Dying Culture" by David F. Wells and Ervin S. Duggan; "The Truths of God's Word" by R. Albert Mohler Jr. and Gene Edward Veith; "Repentance, Recovery, and Confession" by Michael S. Horton and Sinclair B. Ferguson; and "The Reformation of the Church in Doctrine, Worship, and Life" by W. Robert Godfrey and James M. Boice.

The Cambridge Declaration, which followed from the papers, had been prepared in preliminary form by a drafting committee of the alliance, was substantially reworked at the conference on the basis of suggestions and critiques that came from a discussion of the papers, and was then signed formally by nearly all who were present at the closing meeting.

A number of those involved in this meeting had worked together from 1978 to 1988 as part of the International Council on Biblical Inerrancy. But the challenge in Cambridge was far greater than anything the Inerrancy Council had faced. The Inerrancy Council had one clearly defined goal: to recover and defend inerrancy as an essential element in the doctrine of biblical authority and a necessity for the health of the church. Moreover, it was a doctrine on which the majority of evangelicals were supposed to agree. The tasks of the council were: (1) to show that the majority of evangelicals did believe in inerrancy; (2) to explain how inerrancy and the doctrines connected with it are to be understood; and (3) to apply the doctrine to the challenges of that day.

The task facing the alliance is more difficult. First, it is concerned not with one easily defined issue, like inerrancy, but with a pervasive doctrinal downgrade or defection among many alleged evangelicals. Second, this is a matter on which there is no prevailing evangelical consensus. On the contrary, many do not even perceive that there is a problem, which is itself a very large part of the problem. Third, the alliance is seeking to expose and address this vacuum at a time when many churches would claim that their successes show that what the evangelicals are doing is directly on target and that the blessings of God are apparent everywhere. Church services are well attended. Budgets are large. Evangelical books, gospel music, videos, television and radio programs, and seminars are thriving.

So what is wrong with evangelicals? The answer is that we have become worldly. We have abandoned the truths of the Bible and the historic theology of the church, which expresses those truths, and we are trying to do the work of God by means of the world's "theology," wisdom, methods, and agenda instead. Does that mean that evangelicals deny the Bible or have officially turned their backs on classic Christian doctrine? Not necessarily. It is more often the case that the Bible's theology just does not have meaningful bearing on what we think or do—when we understand it, and most of the time we do not. The polls tell us that the gospel most contemporary evangelicals believe in is essentially God helping us to help ourselves. It has a lot to do with self-esteem, good mental attitudes, and worldly success. There is not much preaching about sin, hell, judgment, or the wrath of God, not to mention the great doctrines of the cross such as redemption, atonement, reconciliation, propitiation, justification, grace, and even faith.

Lacking a sound, biblical, and well-understood theology, evangelicals have fallen prey to the pragmatism and consumerism of our times. Instead of calling God's people to worship and serve God, and teaching them how to do it, we treat parishioners as buyers and market the gospel as a "product." A therapeutic worldview has replaced classical Christian categories such as sin and repentance, and many leaders have identified the gospel with such modern idols as a particular political philosophy, psychological views of man, and sociology. To the extent that the doctrines of the Bible no longer guide preaching, teaching, publishing, evangelism, worship, and the daily life of the people of God, to that extent evangelicalism has declined to become a movement that is shaped only by popular whim and sentimentality. To stand in awe of God once again, evangelicals must recognize these idols as idols and confess how much we have been taken captive by them.

The Alliance of Confessing Evangelicals believes that chief among the truths evangelicals need to recover are the great Reformation doctrines summarized by the well-known *sola*'s (Latin for "only"): *sola Scriptura, sola fide, sola gratia, solus Christus,* and *soli Deo gloria.*

Sola Scriptura means "Scripture alone." When they used these words the Reformers were indicating their concern for the Bible's authority, and what they meant to say was that the Bible alone is our ultimate authority—not the pope, not the church, not the traditions of the church or church councils, still less personal intimations or subjective feelings, but Scripture only. These other sources of authority are sometimes useful and may at times have a place, but Scripture alone is ultimate. Therefore, if any of these other authorities differ from Scripture, they are to be judged by the Bible and rejected, rather than it being the other way around. *Sola Scriptura* has been called the formal principle of the Reformation, meaning that it stands at the very beginning and so gives direction and form to all that Christians affirm as Christians.

Evangelicals deny *sola Scriptura* when they reinterpret the Bible to fit in with modern notions of reality and when they ignore its teachings on the basis of supposed private divine revelations or leadings.

Sola fide means "faith alone." When the Reformers used these words they were concerned with the purity of the gospel, wanting to say that believers are justified by God through faith entirely apart from any works they may have done or might do. Justification because of Christ through faith alone became the chief doctrine of the Reformation. *Sola fide* has been called the material principle of the Reformation because it above all others embodies the very matter of the gospel. It is essential to it. Martin Luther called justification by faith the doctrine by which the church stands or falls.

But evangelicals *have* fallen at this point. We have done so by making faith into a work by which we are supposed to bring ourselves into a saving relationship with God or to maintain ourselves in that relationship. We have forgotten that it is the strength of Christ's righteousness, not of the believer's faith, that keeps him or her in a right standing before God.

The Reformers also spoke of *sola gratia,* which means by "grace alone." Here they wanted to insist on the truth that sinners have no claim upon God, that God owes them nothing but punishment for their sins, and that, if he saves them in spite of their sins, which he does in the case of those who are saved, it is only because it pleases him to do it. They taught that salvation is by grace only. By contrast, large numbers of today's evangelicals believe that man is basically good, that God owes everyone a chance to be saved, and that, if we are saved, in the final analysis it is because of our own good decision to receive the Jesus who is offered to us in the gospel.

The Reformers taught that salvation is by and through the work of Jesus Christ only, which is what the slogan *solus Christus* refers to. It means that Jesus has done it all so that now no merit on the part of man, no merit of the saints, no works of ours performed either here or in purgatory can add to that completed saving work.

In fact, any attempt to add to it is a perversion of the gospel and indeed no gospel at all.

To proclaim Christ alone is to proclaim him as the Christian's one and only sufficient Prophet, Priest, and King. We need no other prophets to reveal God's word or will; Jesus has spoken all we need to hear in the Bible. We need no other priests to mediate God's salvation and blessing; Jesus is our one and only mediator. We need no other kings to control the thinking and lives of believers, no gurus; Jesus alone is the king of both individual believers and his church. Jesus is everything to us and for us in the gospel.

Finally, each of these phrases was summed up in the motto *soli Deo gloria*. In Romans 11:36 the words "to him be the glory forever" follow "for from him and through him and to him are all things," meaning that it is because all things really are "from him and through him and to him" that we say, "to God alone be the glory." Do we think about Scripture? It is from God, it has come to us through God's agency, and it will endure forever to God's glory. Justification by faith? It is from God, through God, and to God's glory. Grace? Grace, too, has its source in God, comes to us through the work of God the Son, and is to God's glory.

The site of the April 1996 gathering was significant. Meeting at the Charles Hotel, situated on historic Harvard Square at the very heart of the Harvard University complex, the assembled evangelical leaders were reminded that Harvard's motto is *Veritas* ("truth") and that Harvard as well as many other universities, schools, and colleges were established by our Puritan forbearers as training centers for ministers of the Reformation gospel. They wanted their ministers to be taught the truth of God's Word so that they in turn might teach it to others and thus permeate their world with the truth of the Bible to God's glory.

In the early seventeenth century, when Harvard University was founded, the Puritans were trying to carry on the Reformation. Today we barely have one to carry on, and many have even forgotten what that great spiritual revolution was all about. We need to go back and start again at the very beginning. We need another Reformation.

Years ago, when the International Council on Biblical Inerrancy was in its formative stages, Francis Schaeffer said at an early meeting, "If we do not do something about the departure from a high standard of the Bible on the part of evangelicals, we will not have an evangelical church to pass on to our children." He was right. But today the problem is much worse. If we do not make an effort to "recover and confess the truth of God's Word as did the Reformers," we will not have any church at all to pass on, only an empty religious shell that ignorantly, foolishly, and presumptuously calls itself "evangelical." May God be pleased to spare us that sad possibility, and send a new Reformation.

Cambridge, Massachusetts
April 1996

The Cambridge Declaration

*Evangelical churches today
are increasingly dominated by the spirit of this age
rather than by the Spirit of Christ.
As evangelicals, we call ourselves
to repent of this sin
and to recover the historic Christian faith.*

In the course of history words change. In our day this has happened to the word *evangelical*. In the past it served as a bond of unity between Christians from a wide diversity of church traditions. Historic evangelicalism was confessional. It embraced the essential truths of Christianity as those were defined by the great ecumenical councils of the church. In addition, *evangelicals* also shared a common heritage in the *"sola's"* of the sixteenth-century Protestant Reformation.

Today the light of the Reformation has been significantly dimmed. The consequence is that the word *evangelical* has become so inclusive as to have lost its meaning. We face the peril of losing the unity it has taken centuries to achieve. Because of this crisis and because of our love of Christ, his gospel, and his church, we endeavor to assert anew our commitment to the central truths of the Reformation and of historic evangelicalism. These truths we affirm not because of their role in our traditions, but because we believe that they are central to the Bible.

14

Sola Scriptura: **The Erosion of Authority**

Scripture alone is the inerrant rule of the church's life, but the evangelical church today has separated Scripture from its authoritative function. In practice, the church is guided, far too often, by the culture. Therapeutic technique, marketing strategies, and the beat of the entertainment world often have far more to say about what the church wants, how it functions, and what it offers, than does the Word of God. Pastors have neglected their rightful oversight of worship, including the doctrinal content of the music. As biblical authority has been abandoned in practice, as its truths have faded from Christian consciousness, and as its doctrines have lost their saliency, the church has been increasingly emptied of its integrity, moral authority, and direction.

Rather than adapting Christian faith to satisfy the felt needs of consumers, we must proclaim the Law as the only measure of true righteousness and the gospel as the only announcement of saving truth. Biblical truth is indispensable to the church's understanding, nurture, and discipline.

Scripture must take us beyond our perceived needs to our real needs and liberate us from seeing ourselves through the seductive images, clichés, promises, and priorities of mass culture. It is only in the light of God's truth that we understand ourselves aright and see God's provision for our need. The Bible, therefore, must be taught and preached in the church. Sermons must be expositions of the Bible and its teachings, not expressions of the preacher's opinions or the ideas of the age. We must settle for nothing less than what God has given.

The work of the Holy Spirit in personal experience cannot be disengaged from Scripture. The Spirit does not speak in ways that are independent of Scripture. Apart from Scripture we would never have known of God's grace in Christ. The biblical Word, rather than spiritual experience, is the test of truth.

Thesis 1: **Sola Scriptura**

We reaffirm the inerrant Scripture to be the sole source of written divine revelation, which alone can bind the conscience. The Bible alone teaches all that is necessary for our salvation from sin and is the standard by which all Christian behavior must be measured.

We deny that any creed, council, or individual may bind a Christian's conscience, that the Holy Spirit speaks independently of or contrary to what is set forth in the Bible, or that personal spiritual experience can ever be a vehicle of revelation.

Solus Christus: The Erosion of Christ-Centered Faith

As evangelical faith has become secularized, its interests have been blurred with those of the culture. The result is a loss of absolute values, permissive individualism, and a substitution of wholeness for holiness, recovery for repentance, intuition for truth, feeling for belief, chance for providence, and immediate gratification for enduring hope. Christ and his cross have moved from the center of our vision.

Thesis 2: Solus Christus

We reaffirm that our salvation is accomplished by the mediatorial work of the historical Christ alone. His sinless life and substitutionary atonement alone are sufficient for our justification and reconciliation to the Father.

We deny that the gospel is preached if Christ's substitutionary work is not declared and faith in Christ and his work is not solicited.

Sola Gratia: The Erosion of the Gospel

Unwarranted confidence in human ability is a product of fallen human nature. This false confidence now fills the evangelical world—from the self-esteem gospel to the health and wealth gospel, from those who have transformed the gospel into a product to be sold and sinners into consumers who want to buy, to others who treat Christian faith as being true simply because it works. This silences the doctrine of justification regardless of the official commitments of our churches.

God's grace in Christ is not merely necessary but is the sole efficient cause of salvation. We confess that human beings are born spiritually dead and are incapable even of cooperating with regenerating grace.

Thesis 3: Sola Gratia

We reaffirm that in salvation we are rescued from God's wrath by his grace alone. It is the supernatural work of the Holy Spirit that brings us to Christ by releasing us from our bondage to sin and raising us from spiritual death to spiritual life.

We deny that salvation is in any sense a human work. Human methods, techniques, or strategies by themselves cannot accomplish this transformation. Faith is not produced by our unregenerated human nature.

Sola Fide: The Erosion of the Chief Article

Justification is by grace alone through faith alone because of Christ alone. This is the article by which the church stands or falls. Today this article is often ignored, distorted, or sometimes even denied by leaders, scholars, and pastors who claim to be evangelical. Although fallen human nature has always recoiled from recognizing its need for Christ's imputed righteousness, modernity greatly fuels the fires of this discontent with the biblical gospel. We have allowed this discontent to dictate the nature of our ministry and what it is we are preaching.

Many in the church growth movement believe that sociological understanding of those in the pew is as important to the success of the gospel as is the biblical truth which is proclaimed. As a result, theological convictions are frequently divorced from the work of the ministry. The marketing orientation in many churches takes this even further, erasing the distinction between the biblical Word and the world, robbing Christ's cross of its offense, and reducing Christian faith to the principles and methods which bring success to secular corporations.

While the theology of the cross may be believed, these movements are actually emptying it of its meaning. There is no gospel except that of Christ's substitution in our place whereby God imputed to him our sin and imputed to us his righteousness. Because he bore our judgment, we now walk in his grace as those who are forever pardoned, accepted, and adopted as God's children. There is no basis for our acceptance before God except in Christ's saving work, not in our patriotism, churchly devotion, or moral decency. The gospel declares what God has done for us in Christ. It is not about what we can do to reach him.

Thesis 4: Sola Fide

We reaffirm that justification is by grace alone through faith alone because of Christ alone. In justification Christ's righteousness is imputed to us as the only possible satisfaction of God's perfect justice. *We deny* that justification rests on any merit to be found in us, or upon the grounds of an infusion of Christ's righteousness in us, or that an institution claiming to be a church that denies or condemns *sola fide* can be recognized as a legitimate church.

Soli Deo Gloria: The Erosion of God-Centered Worship

Wherever in the church biblical authority has been lost, Christ has been displaced, the gospel has been distorted, or faith has been perverted, it has always been for one reason: Our interests have displaced God's and we are doing his work in our way. The loss of God's centrality in the life of today's church is common and lamentable. It is this loss that allows us to transform worship into entertainment, gospel preaching into marketing, believing into technique, being good into feeling good about ourselves, and faithfulness into being successful. As a result, God, Christ, and the Bible have come to mean too little to us and rest too inconsequentially upon us.

God does not exist to satisfy human ambitions, cravings, the appetite for consumption, or our own private spiritual interests. We must focus on God in our worship, rather than the satisfaction of our personal needs. God is sovereign in worship; we are not. Our concern must be for God's kingdom, not our own empires, popularity, or success.

Thesis 5: Soli Deo Gloria

We reaffirm that because salvation is of God and has been accomplished by God, it is for God's glory and that we must glorify him always. We must live our entire lives before the face of God, under the authority of God, and for his glory alone.

We deny that we can properly glorify God if our worship is confused with entertainment, if we neglect either Law or Gospel in our preaching, or if self-improvement, self-esteem, or self-fulfillment are allowed to become alternatives to the gospel.

A Call to Repentance and Reformation

The faithfulness of the evangelical church in the past contrasts sharply with its unfaithfulness in the present. Earlier in this century, evangelical churches sustained a remarkable missionary endeavor and built many religious institutions to serve the cause of biblical truth and Christ's kingdom. That was a time when Christian behavior and expectations were markedly different from those in the culture. Today they often are not. The evangelical world today is losing its biblical fidelity, moral compass, and missionary zeal.

We repent of our worldliness. We have been influenced by the "gospels" of our secular culture, which are no gospels. We have weakened the church by our own lack of serious repentance, our blindness to the sins in ourselves which we see so clearly in others, and our inexcusable failure adequately to tell others about God's saving work in Jesus Christ.

We also earnestly call back erring professing evangelicals who have deviated from God's Word in the matters discussed in this declaration. This includes those who declare that there is hope of eternal life apart from explicit faith in Jesus Christ, who claim that those who reject Christ in this life will be annihilated rather than endure the just judgment of God through eternal suffering, or who claim that evangelicals and Roman Catholics are one in Jesus Christ even where the biblical doctrine of justification is not believed.

The Alliance of Confessing Evangelicals asks all Christians to give consideration to implementing this declaration in the church's worship, ministry, policies, life, and evangelism.

For Christ's sake. Amen.

Alliance of Confessing Evangelicals
Cambridge, Massachusetts
April 20, 1996

Contributors

James Montgomery Boice
Senior pastor, Tenth Presbyterian Church, Philadelphia, Pennsylvania.

Ervin S. Duggan
President and CEO, Public Broadcasting Service, Washington, D.C.

Sinclair B. Ferguson
Professor of theology, Westminster Theological Seminary, Philadelphia, Pennsylvania.

W. Robert Godfrey
President and professor of theology, Westminster Theological Seminary, Escondido, California.

Michael S. Horton
President, Christians United for Reformation, Anaheim, California.

R. Albert Mohler Jr.
President, Southern Baptist Theological Seminary, Louisville, Kentucky.

Gene Edward Veith
Dean of the School of Arts and Sciences, Concordia University, Mequon, Wisconsin.

David F. Wells
Andrew Mutch Distinguished Professor of Theology, Gordon-Conwell Theological Seminary, South Hamilton, Massachusetts.

We are calling the church,

amidst our dying culture,

to repent of its worldliness,

to recover and confess the truth

of God's Word

as did the Reformers,

and to see that truth embodied

in doctrine, worship, and life.

1

Our Dying Culture

David F. Wells

What is striking about our culture today is that its corruption is not simply at the edges. It is not simply found among the cultured elite, the New Class that stands at the gates of our national institutions to bar entry to those whose views are judged to be intolerable. It is not simply found among postmodern academics who are bent upon overturning all meaning and moral principle, or among vicious street gangs, or among rappers who spew forth obscenities and violence, or among the venders of pornography, or in the bizarre and unashamed revelations of deeply private matters that are aired on television talk shows. What is striking is that this corruption is ubiquitous. It is not located in this or that pocket of depravity, but is spread like a dense fog throughout our society. It is even spread by those who are safe, ordinary, dull, and dim-witted, and not merely by the incendiary and bellicose, the subversive and anti-social. "Wherever one looks," writes Robert Bork, "the traditional virtues of this culture are being lost, its vices multiplied, its values degraded—in short, the culture itself is unraveling."[1] And the American public apparently agrees with this diagnosis. An overwhelming majority, 90 percent, believes that America is slipping ever deeper into a "moral decline."

The Moral Majority

This undoing of our society can be grasped quickly by looking at a few raw statistics that signal the presence of the deep and destructive pathologies that are at work. Since 1960 population has increased by 41 percent while violent crime has risen 560 percent.[2] The U.S. Department of Justice projects that eight out of ten people will be the victims of violent crime at least once in their lives. And the most active incubator for this violence is in the ten to seventeen age group, where the rate of the perpetration of violent crime has soared 400 percent since 1960. Since 1960 illegitimacy has increased 400 percent.[3] In 1990, 65.2 percent of black children were born to unmarried mothers. And since *Roe v. Wade* legalized abortion in 1973, an estimated 28 million unborn children have lost their lives. Since 1960 the rate of teen suicides has risen more than 200 percent, making it the third leading cause of death among these young people.[4] Since 1960 the divorce rate has increased 200 percent; as a consequence, less than 60 percent of children live with both biological parents. And while spending on our public schools has more than doubled in constant dollars since 1960, SAT scores have dropped, on average, seventy-five points. The federal tax burden on families with children is now 24 percent of their income, whereas in 1960, when children were doing better in school and better in society, the federal government only asked for 12 percent of family income.[5] These facts diminish the hope that we can simply buy our way out of our predicament with larger and larger public outlays.

These, however, are the statistics that are graphic. Just as telling, and perhaps of more interest, are those that measure more private matters, such as our moral intentions, matters that may not always be matters of law.

Americans today, say James Patterson and Peter Kim, "stand alone in a way unknown to any previous generation."[6] They are alone, not least, because they are without any objective moral compass. "The religious figures and Scriptures that gave us rules for so many centuries, the political system which gave us laws, all have lost their meaning in our moral imagination."[7] While the great majority of Americans believe that they actually keep the Ten Commandments, only 13 percent think that each of these commandments has moral validity. It is no surprise to learn that 74 percent say that they will steal without compunction, 64 percent say that they will lie if there is an advantage to be had, 53 percent say that, given a chance, they will commit adultery, 41 percent say that they intend to use recreational drugs, and 30 percent say that they will cheat on their taxes. What may be the clearest indicator of the disappearance of a moral texture to society is the loss of shame. While 86 percent admit to lying regularly to their parents, 75 percent to a friend, 73 percent to a sibling, and 73 percent to a lover, only 11 percent cited lying as having produced a serious level of shame. While 74 percent will steal without compunction, only 9 percent register any significant shame. While pornography has blossomed into a $21 billion industry that accounts for a quarter of all the videos rented in shops, in the thriving hotel business, and on cable, only 2 percent experience guilt about watching them.[8] And, not surprisingly, at the center of this slide into moral relativism is the disappearance of God. Only 17 percent define sin as a violation of God's will.

The moral terrain that was once dominated by a set of beliefs and virtues to which wide public assent was given has now disappeared. There are, no doubt, many reasons for this. Aside from anything else, the massive waves of immigrants, legal and otherwise, in this century have changed our nation. In 1990 the Census discovered in America three hundred races, six hundred Indian tribes, and seventy different Hispanic groups. As our social diversity has expanded, our national unity has been weakened[9] and our consensus about what is right and wrong has crumbled. But secularization, in particular, has decimated this consensus, and today not only is the public square stripped of divine meaning but so, too, is human consciousness. Amid all of the abundance and the technological marvels of our time, what is true and what is right have lost their hold upon our society. They have lost their saliency, their capacity to shape life. Today, our moral center is gone. It is not merely that secularization has marginalized God, relegating him to the outer edges of our public life from whence he becomes entirely irrelevant, but we have also lost our understanding of ourselves as moral beings. In our private universe, as in that which is public, there is no center.

At the most obvious level this is suggested by the fact that 67 percent of Americans do not believe in moral absolutes—that is, in moral norms that are enduring and are applicable to all people in all places and all times—and 70 percent do not believe in truth that is similarly absolute.[10] What this means, then, is that running through our society is a San Andreas fault line of a moral kind, one that may be engaged initially at the level of conflicting values but which also, and at the same time, involves competing worldviews, for one part of our society believes in absolutes and the other does not. And since the great majority of Americans do not believe in absolutes, Jerry Falwell was guilty of considerable chutzpa in calling his movement the Moral Majority.

Among the real moral majority today it is not hard to discern pagan motifs. Camille Paglia notes, with respect to pop culture, that it represents "an eruption of the never-defeated paganism of the West."[11] Her thesis, which she developed in *Sexual Personae,* is that there are always in culture two principles at work, the Apollonian and the Dionysian—one whose urge is to expand and the other whose work is to restrain, one that undoes shape and the other that demands definition. What is now expanding, what she believes was recovered in the 1960s, is the pagan impulse, now wrapped in what is earthy and sensual. This, happily, is liberating us from all social taboos.[12]

"For me," she continues, "the ultimate power in the universe is nature, not God, whose existence I can understand only as depersonalized energy."[13] Defying many of the icons of feminist devotion, she then sets out with brilliant and pristine clarity what it means today to be pagan, and she is far more mainstream than the feminist critics who take such pained exception to her. Pornography, for example, she thinks is good. "Porn dreams of eternal fires of desire, without fatigue, incapacity, aging, or death. What feminists denounce as woman's humiliating total accessibility in porn is actually her elevation to high priestess of a pagan paradise garden, where the body has become a bountiful fruit tree and where growth and harvest is simultaneous." She adds that "'dirt' is contamination to the Christian but fertile loam to the pagan."[14] Paglia, to be sure, is cutting her own path through the world with a kind of beguiling swagger, but many of her assumptions, which she rightly calls pagan, are very widely held.

Indeed, they are even seeping into the church in milder and disguised forms. In 1993, for example, women from several mainline denominations met in Minneapolis under the auspices of the World Council of Churches to explore the sexual side of God. Their erotically charged language, which produced no small furor, also gave unmistakable evidence of the reappearance of what looks quite like the old Baal fertility rites, dressed up though they are in modern, Christian form.[15] And, more generally, Carl Braaten and Robert Jenson are surely correct in seeing a neo-pagan influence evident in the current fascination in the churches in mining the self for religious meaning, an undertaking based on the assumption that salvation consists in getting in touch with oneself. The result is a faith that is neither about truth nor unique. It is, further, devoid of cognitive substance, and its Christ, who is divorced from history, has become simply a mold into which modern therapeutic content is poured.[16] These are the contemporary garments in which the old paganism now strolls our world.

This resurgent paganism poses an enormous challenge, one that is both cultural and churchly. In this chapter, however, I focus on only a small part of it. I contend that the loss of our moral center, which is one of its chief consequences, is at the heart of the unraveling in our society. Its final and most destructive outcome, which is now upon us, is that we have lost our ability to discern between, or even to talk meaningfully about, Good and Evil. And while this collapse into cynicism and moral chaos bodes poorly for the future of American life, it is opening opportunities for the Christian faith that have not been present in this way at least during the twentieth century and, perhaps, for an even greater period.

Obedience to the Unenforceable

The cultural accord that has shaped our past was actually a matter of tough and deliberate virtue. This virtue lay in our simple insistence among ourselves that we would preserve three domains in society. Lying between law on the one side, and freedom on the other, would be a middle territory for the cultivation of character and the affirmation of truth, one that would be as vital to the preservation of our society as law and freedom. This accord, to be sure, now seems quite quaint following the postmodern assault on all virtue and meaning. But, as we shall see, that assault has not been without a very steep price.

Today we are experiencing the competition between law and freedom to occupy this middle territory. The result is that the fires of license are stoked constantly by our growing moral relativism while at the same time they have to be constantly doused by our resort to law and government. We live precariously on the knife edge between chaos and control, for what was once an open space between law and freedom, one governed by character and truth, is now deserted. The result is that freedom is now unfettered and law must do double duty by assuming the role of character. That seems to be the best way to understand many of the cultural strains, the turmoil and disarray, which mark our time.

Of course it is the case that every society needs laws as well as the weight of the judicial system to enforce those laws. In every society there are flagrant violators who rob, swindle, beat, and massacre, and it is by a rather simple calculus that society acts. It acts against the violator to issue just desert, to protect itself from being ravaged further, and, perhaps, to offer a corrective toward reforming the wrongdoer.

Along with establishing the right of law, the Constitution also secures a large role for freedom in our society. It secures for its citizenry freedom from unwarranted intrusion by the state into both private and public life. The Constitution is less clear about what we are free *for,* than what we are free *from,* but that itself may be part of its genius. It is because we are free from state tyranny that originality and creativity and, indeed, Christian believing have all been able to flourish in America.

Lying between law and freedom, however, has always been this third domain. It is that of character, the practice of private virtue such as honesty, decency, the telling of truth, and all the other kinds of moral obligation. It is that of public virtue such as civic duty, social responsibility, philanthropy, the articulation of great ideals and good policies, all those things that might be encompassed in Paul's statement that the Gentiles, "who have not the law, do by nature things required by the law" (Rom. 2:14). This third domain is what must regulate life in the absence of legal coercion and government regulation. It is where law and restraint are *self*-imposed. The demands come from within, not from without. In this area we find what John Silber has called "obedience to the unenforceable," which was the language of English jurist John Fletcher Moulton earlier this century, who went on to say: "The real greatness of a nation, its true civilization, is measured by the extent of this land of obedience to the unenforceable. It measures the extent to which the nation trusts its citizens, and its area testifies to the way they behave in response to that trust."[17]

Today the middle territory is shrinking daily as our understanding of ourselves as moral beings collapses, and it is being invaded by the two other domains. It is this fact that raises the most profound questions about American life. Law must now do what church, family, character, belief, and even cultural expectations once did. What is going to happen, then, if we keep stoking the fires of our rampant, amoral individualism and have to keep dousing those fires with greater and greater recourse to litigation and regulation? Our society is going to become a platform on which more and more collisions occur. It is going to be host to more and more thwarted, frustrated, and impeded desires. And how will this be resolved? Should we expect greater chaos or greater control in the future? The answer, of course, depends on how our freedom, now channeled through our individualism, and how our legal system, established by the Constitution, choreograph their ballet. Only a few illustrations of this dynamic can, of course, be offered, first from the side of freedom and then from that of law.

An Ode to Myself

Freedom today is largely understood through the prism of our individualism. Individualism comes in all shades, but Robert Bellah's distinction between that which is utilitarian and that which is expressive is one that is widely accepted.[18] The former has to do with the calculations of career, of the individual pursuit of gain and advantage in the workplace. The latter is more psychological than commercial. It is also a reflex to the harsh competition that capitalism produces. This reflex takes the form of seeking liberty from all constraints and, in consumption and leisure, finding solace for the wounds the soul absorbed at the workplace. These are the psychological compensations for the brutalities of the work week.

This reflex, then, carries with it a sense of entitlement to being left alone, to being able to live in a way that is emancipated from the demands and expectations of others, to being able to fashion one's own life the way one wants to, to being able to develop one's own values and beliefs in one's own way, to being able to resist all authority. To be free in these ways, we think, is indispensable to being a true individual. And much has happened to this ideal from the time when Tocqueville described and admired it (the nineteenth century) and what we find in its outworking today.

Nineteenth-century individualism was one in which personal responsibility played a large role. It was the kind in which people thought for themselves, provided for themselves, owed nothing, and usually worked out their independence within a community, loosely defined though some of these were. This produced the kind of person who, in David Riesman's language, was "inner-directed," that is, who was guided by an internal gyroscope of character and belief and who, as a result, saw it as a virtue to have clear goals, to work hard, to live by ethical principles, and who probably admired those who had taken lonely stands and triumphed over adversity by inner fortitude. This, says Riesman, is the kind of person who would rather be right than be president.

Today's individualist would rather be president than be right. It is not character that defines the way individualism functions today, but emancipation from values, from community, and from the past in order to pursue gain, of one kind or another, in the present.

"The freedom of our day," declared a Harvard valedictorian, "is the freedom to devote ourselves to any values we please, on the mere condition that we do not believe them to be true."[19]

Today, it is not ideology that poses the greatest danger to America but what Zbigniew Brzezinski calls "permissive cornucopia." His argument is that following the spectacular failure of twentieth-century totalitarianisms, and the rise of democracy worldwide, the United States is now the world's leader. Yet whether it will be able to discharge its responsibilities has become doubtful because of its rotting fabric. He sees a society "in which the progressive decline in the centrality of moral criteria is matched by heightened preoccupation with material and sensual gratification."[20] This produces deep undercurrents of hedonism in which personal gratification is pursued regardless of the good of society.

The game of "Monopoly," Parker Brothers' enormously successful creation and a favorite since the Depression, really is a metaphor for Our Time. Each player begins with the same amount of money and then, by a combination of chance (which lands him or her on desirable properties that can be purchased), calculation (whether or not to buy and build, thus placing the other players in jeopardy should they land on the property), and misfortune (which lands one on someone else's property), the game moves to its end by an inexorable logic no player can effect. The buying and selling is made possible by the flow of money from the bank, but this is controlled in such a way that survival is assured to no one and, in the end, only one player ultimately survives. Here are all of the elements of modern life: Here are the inexorable laws of the marketplace, which, Bellah notes, are "absolute but amoral";[21] here is life's ruthlessness and unpredictability, for in the end there is only one survivor; here players try to get away with what they can, as they do in life, for no player, landing on someone else's property, will articulate that fact if the other player has not noticed; and here, as is so often the case in life, there is no place for the virtues, no place for mercy if someone is unable to pay rent, no place for compassion for those about to lose everything, no place, in fact, for anyone but oneself. This is modern life.

The margin contains the handwritten note: *Secular Therapy*

The autonomy to devise one's own values, however, is precisely why contemporary individualists do not find connections to the world. They are, Riesman says, "ignoring those issues of related-ness to others and commitment to keep intact the precarious struc-ture of civilization,"[22] and this is partly why therapists have come to assume such a large role in our culture. What they try to do is to enable the self to make the adjustments necessary to find meaning in and connections to life, but this is often done under the language of enhancing the self, of enabling it to transcend itself, rather than that of limiting itself through moral obligation, service, self-sacri-fice, and commitment to others. The therapist, in other words, is looking at life in ways that are, as Bellah argues, "generally hostile to the older ideas of moral order." Why is this? The answer, of course, is that technique has supplanted moral discourse, and the manipulation of the self has itself become the new (secular) reli-gious order. Psychology is religion.

And in the public realm what this means is that personality has come to supplant character in importance. We as individuals sell our personalities in the workplace as commodities that are discon-nected from the inner lives in which they arose. The same is true of television. After all, who knows what vices and character flaws, what beliefs and values, lie behind the image we see on the screen of a person who is charming, relaxed, and funny? We know that person only as charming, relaxed, and funny, and not as he or she may be—rapacious, promiscuous, conniving, and deceitful.[23] There is a bull market today for image and personality as commodities that are separable from the person.

Nowhere is this disengagement between personality and char-acter more plain than in the way that celebrities have replaced heroes in our culture, and in the way that villains have disappeared. A hero was someone who embodied what people prized but did so in such a way that others wanted to emulate him or her.[24] A celebrity may also want to be emulated, but the grounds of the emulation have now changed. A celebrity usually embodies nothing and is usually only known for being known. Fame, in our world of images and manipulation, can be manufactured with little or no accomplish-ment behind it but it cannot be emulated as can the virtue that a hero embodies. In Daniel Boorstin's rather caustic comparison: "The hero was distinguished by his achievement; the celebrity by his image or trademark. The hero created himself; the celebrity is created by the media. The hero was a big man; the celebrity is a big name."[25] It is our *commercial* culture that produces the celebrity, but it was the *moral* culture that, more often than not, elevated the hero. As celebrities replace heroes, image replaces character, and commercial culture replaces that which is moral, we are left with a kind of individualism that simply festers with lawlessness because moral character is not its central interest. Indeed, it is not an interest at all.

In 1995 Calvin Klein tested public sentiment by airing some advertisements that featured adolescents in sexually provocative poses. The public—or, at least, that part of it that was vocal—was not quite ready for this, nor was the Justice Department, which began to ponder whether child pornography laws had been broken. The advertisements were eventually withdrawn. However, as John Leo pointed out,[26] not only were these advertisements treading a well-worn path of using sex to sell products, but they were also being pitched to the spirit of lawlessness in the culture at which many other advertisers are also aiming. This is the spirit that assumes that there should be no obstacles to the expression of any instinctual urge, that people should be able to do whatever they want to do, that there should be no moral constraints. This is the surfacing in the 1990s of the 1960s radicalism with its antisocial and antimorality impulse, which Paglia celebrates, but now it is considerably Yuppiefied. The early pioneers were Nike's "Just Do It!" (in other words, don't think about it and don't let anything stand in the way to your doing it) and Burger King's "Sometimes, you gotta break the rules." And the imitators have been numerous. Bacardi Black rum, which advertises itself as "the taste of the night," goes on to say, "Some people embrace the night because rules of the day do not apply." Easy Spirit shoes even latched onto this theme, promising a shoe that "conforms to your foot so you don't have to conform to anything." Ralph Lauren's Safari celebrates "living without boundaries"; even stayed and reliable Merril Lynch declares that "Your world should know no boundaries"; and Nieman Marcus encourages its customers to relax because, it says, there are "No rules here."

It is, then, this moral space between law and freedom that shrinks daily, for what cannot be enforced, it is now assumed, should not be a matter of obedience. This, in itself, is a recipe for profound social disorder, but its most pernicious outcome, the one that has the deepest effects, is one hardly noticed at all. It is that we have lost our ability to talk about Good and Evil.

This, in fact, is a deficiency long in the making, but one whose size and importance have been much enlarged in recent decades. Andrew Delbanco places the beginnings of the problem well back into the nineteenth century. He notes the dismemberment of the self that occurred as industrialization reshaped the country. We lost our sense of "we" in community, which was replaced by the lonely "I." The older kind of world in which God ruled sovereignly and presided over its moral order became seriously fractured. To soldiers involved in the Civil War, for example, and to the nation as it watched, it was a matter of blind chance who survived and who did not. To pray for grace increasingly became more embarrassing than to hope for luck. Sin, by the end of the nineteenth century, was rapidly fading as a belief, and how could it have been otherwise, he asks. "Sin, after all, means transgression against God. But God had been replaced by fortune, and fortune makes no moral judgments. . . . In what amounted to a new paganism, the concept of evil devolved into bad luck, and 'good luck' became the new benediction."[27]

The loss of moral centeredness, a loss occasioned by the disappearance of God, by the supplanting of providence by chance and of moral purpose by self-interest, changed everything. It changed the meaning of death, since there was no one to whom the dying were going. And it changed the meaning of life, since what had given it meaning had now gone. Writing as early as 1929, Walter Lippmann described the "modern man" as having

> moments of blank misgiving in which he finds that the civilization of which he is a part leaves a dusty taste in his mouth. He may be very busy with many things, but he discovers one day that he is no longer sure they are worth doing. He has been much preoccupied; but he is no longer sure he knows why. He has become involved in

"I am ?"

an elaborate routine of pleasures; and they do not seem to amuse him very much. He finds it hard to believe that doing any one thing is better than doing any other thing, or, in fact, that it is better than doing nothing at all.[28]

Americans had been slow to see that as the old moral map faded they would be left, not with an alternative, but with no map at all. It is true that the neo-orthodox theologians, like Reinhold Niebuhr, tried to staunch the flow in moral understanding and bring about a more realistic understanding of human nature. They did have a few moments of success, but these turned out to be quite fleeting. The real story of our time was being told through the relentless march of secular rationality as it destroyed all before it. Today, Delbanco says, it has left moderns with only one conclusion: "to acknowledge that no story about the intrinsic meaning of the world has universal validity."[29]

It is this cruel irony that we have brought upon ourselves. The Enlightenment, which substituted its own rationality for God's revelation, its purpose for his, its vision for his truth, its norms for his laws, now finds itself attacked by its own postmodern progeny and the great overthrower is itself overthrown. In an ironic replay of Samson's life, the disaffected children of the Enlightenment, those who have tagged along behind its proud dreamers, now find themselves in painful captivity, their eyes gouged out, and in one last spasm of rebellion encircle the pillars of Enlightenment ideology itself and collapse the whole structure upon themselves. But even as they die, they know that in a world ruled only by chance, this final act has no meaning either.

As our understanding of ourselves as moral beings has disappeared, the vacuum has now been filled by alternative anthropologies. These alternatives, however, are not only at the center of our cultural crisis; they are also at the center of our identity crisis. If we are not moral beings, who stand in the presence of God and before his Law, who are we? "I am my genes," we reply; "I am my sexual orientation"; "I am my past"; "I am my self-image"; "I am my personality"; "I am my experiences"; "I am what I have"; "I am what I eat"; "I am what I do"; "I am who I know." This bravado echoes with its own emptiness. Sin has vanished, but quite plainly this throw of the dice has not won the game. Not only are our personal dilemmas growing exponentially, but our culture is also falling apart.

The more we indulge our moral and spiritual illusions, the more we have to douse the consequences by resorting more and more to law and litigation and the more we have to find palliatives for our own boredom, cynicism, and despair.

You Are Being Watched

If our freedom has led us into the dead end of license and nihilism, it is law that must now rescue us. Since the 1960s, Gregory Sisk says, "a vision of the federal judiciary as the moral tutor appointed for a recalcitrant society has become dominant in the American legal academy and increasingly in the courts themselves."[30] Thus it is that the courts have taken it upon themselves to elevate certain values and to discount others, an obvious case being the creation of a legal right, and the granting of moral permission, for abortion in *Roe v. Wade*. And later, in the 1992 *Planned Parenthood v. Casey* case, three justices on the Supreme Court suggested that the acceptance of this moral principle was required as a matter of good citizenship. The Constitution intended that the courts would provide a small part of social morality, but in the dwindling world of the "obedience to the unenforceable," the courts now threaten to provide the only morality there is, and some of it, at least, has become questionable.

The courts, in fact, have engaged our society across the entire spectrum of its life, from the most insignificant matters to the most weighty. In February 1996—to take an instance of the most insignificant—Antonina Pevnev, the mother of a three-year-old girl, received a restraining order from Judge Charles Spurlock of the Suffolk Superior Court in Boston against the three-year-old son of Margaret Inge. Apparently these two toddlers had a spat in the sandbox and the court had to issue its injunction in order to preserve the peace at Charles River Park playground.[31] Is it romantic to suppose that the earlier social arrangements for resolving such disputes were superior? In this case, the mothers would have had a go at it constrained by some sense of propriety and moral obligation. If they had failed, the fathers, then the neighbors, then the neighborhood, then the respective ministers. Character, custom, reputation, a sense of social obligation all would have acted to douse the conflict and prevent it from erupting any further. Today, however, what all of these agencies once did, Judge Spurlock was obliged to provide through the court.

It was inevitable that a culture that nourishes 70 percent of the world's lawyers would be the one that would attempt to convert every desire into a right. And certainly the courts have encouraged this development by widening constitutional guarantees to free speech to encompass freedom from unwarranted search and seizure, reproductive freedom and, somewhat more sporadically, the rights of all to equal education and equal opportunity. The great benefit of a right is that, once established in law, it cannot be overturned. A right lodged in the Constitution is a right that government is pledged to defend, regardless of the financial and social costs and without respect for the size of the opposition to the possession of that right. Rights are therefore eminently desirable things to have, especially in a culture that is spinning into license and lawlessness, for a right provides a social defense that character once, without the law's coercion, provided for others as a matter of conscience.

Multiculturalism in the 1960s was initially an expression of the Civil Rights Movement. It sought to allow visibility to women and ethnic minorities who had been excluded from positions of power and influence in society. It sought to welcome cultural differences and to see in these differences what would enrich, rather than impoverish, the country. It was an argument that some advanced from Christian premises and others on the Enlightenment principles of liberty, equality, and justice for all. Multiculturalism today, however, has largely lost its ideals, given our postmodern context, and it has rapidly degenerated simply into a search for group power. What accompanies this is not the embrace of other cultures but an ugly censoriousness toward all those with whom it is in disagreement. Ironically, multiculturalism today is not about culture at all but about politics and power and what Richard Bernstein calls the "dictatorship of virtue."[32]

In 1995 the University of Massachusetts, following a number of other universities,[33] proposed a policy on harassment that went well beyond the constitutional safeguards of citizenship. This policy was designed to disallow certain kinds of speech with respect to women and ethnic minorities, to students who were pregnant, those who had the HIV virus, those who were gay, student cultural practices, the language they spoke, and their political affiliation. Apparently, students would be vulnerable to the university's sanction if they expressed judgments about the morality of homosexuality, or if they opposed someone's political viewpoint too vigorously, or if they snickered when they heard that someone was pregnant. This proposed law was made necessary because tolerance had vanished on campus. When moral principle breaks down, of course, we are left with no other recourse than that of law. Do we not have to wonder, though, whether placing all our social marbles in the basket of legal constraint is not worse than the problem it was designed to solve?

But what is the alternative? The alternative, unfortunately, is usually the evasion of moral responsibility. For on the underside of this multiculturalism is the cultivation of victimhood. This is at the confluence of the deep currents of individualism, the therapeutic framework in which we think, and the loss of the moral fabric to life. "The ethos of victimization," writes Charles Sykes, "has an endless capacity not only for exculpating one's self from blame, washing away responsibility in a torrent of explanation—racism, sexism, rotten parents, addiction, and illness—but also for projecting guilt onto others."[34] This "depersonalization of blame" is a sure symptom of the decay in our character and the loss of our older moral vision.

Today we stand at the turbulent meeting place of these two swirling, swollen currents. From one side, the loss of moral vision threatens to undo culture along its entire front; from the other side comes the escalating recourse to law in order to contain a society that is splitting its own seams. This contest between license and law is one that, in the absence of recovered moral fiber, can only become more shrill, more frustrating, more culturally destabilizing, more damaging, and more dangerous, and it is one that poses both temptations and opportunities to Christian faith.

The temptations will be there if we fail to understand this dynamic clearly. Since the task of building character is so hard, the recovery of this third domain so daunting, the recourse to law, and the coercion that political triumph might allow, is almost irresistible. No political agenda, however, can restore what has most been lost, this "obedience to the unenforceable." We can pass laws against murder, but not against hatred; against adultery, but not against lust; against fraud, but not against lying. We can condemn violence, but we cannot command kindness. We can condemn intolerance, but we cannot require civility.

It is this cultural dilemma that now drives the debate between Democrats and Republicans, the one wanting more law and the other more freedom, and we need to say, with respect, that both parties are both right and wrong. Republicans are right that government regulation is burdensome and sometimes ineffective, but they are slow to see the consequences of having less law in a culture whose moral character is worn, where "obedience to the unenforceable" is tepid. Democrats are right to fear what will happen in such a society where the heavy hand of the law is lifted, but they rarely see that the law cannot restore what we have lost, which is our sense of "obedience to the unenforceable." Republicans ask for more freedom, Democrats for more law, but freedom in the absence of public virtue is as disastrous as more law because of the absence of public virtue.

If these are the worst of times, they are also the best of times, for a moment of unprecedented opportunity is opening before the church. It is, therefore, a matter of some poignancy to realize that in the very moment when our culture is plunging into unprecedented darkness, at the very moment in which it is most vulnerable, and in which the soil is most ready for the gospel, the evangelical church has lost its nerve. At the very moment when boldness and courage are called for, what we see, all too often, is timidity and cowardice. Instead of confronting modernity, the church is capitulating to it. The gospel we should be preaching is one that offers an alternative to our cultural darkness; what the church is preaching is a gospel that too often reflects that cultural darkness. Because therapeutic language has often replaced that which is moral and the quest for wholeness has taken the place of holiness, sin has become dysfunction and salvation has become recovery. It is a gospel more about self-sufficiency than about Christ's unique sufficiency, and it goes hand in hand with churches that prize marketing success above moral and spiritual authenticity.

The loss of moral categories in our society has also transformed the search for what is spiritual outside the church. In what many see as a surprising twist, our deeply secularized world is now also awash with spiritualities of almost every conceivable kind. What so many have in common, however, is that they are offering spiritual benefits with little or no accountability. Designer religion of the 1990s allows itself to be tailored to each personality. It gives but never takes; it satisfies inner needs but never asks for repentance; it offers mystery and asks for no service. It provides a sense of Something Other in life but never requires that we stand before that Other.

This yearning for what is spiritual amid our secular wasteland is surely testimony to the fact that, as Augustine put it, we were formed by God and our hearts are restless until they find their rest in him. Not even the torrent of modernity, with all of its anxiety, cynicism, and moral confusion, has succeeded in erasing what we are by virtue of our creation.

The truth is that the fields have never been so ready for harvesting. Our culture has never been riper to hear a Word about a God large enough to provide meaning rooted in his own transcendent character and forgiveness that is objective because of Christ's cross. Without knowing why, many today ache to hear such things. This is no time for the evangelical world to lose its nerve. It is a time to recover a faith strong and virile enough to offer to our culture the alternative that it needs to hear.

2

The Living Church

Ervin S. Duggan

o dire is the state of the American culture as it slouches toward the end of the twentieth century, that even the most lurid description of its moral, intellectual, and spiritual decay is likely to seem understated. The nation's urban streets and its popular media explode with violence. Underage drinking and an epidemic of drug use swamp law enforcement agencies and treatment centers. Teenage pregnancies feed triple epidemics of abortion, illegitimacy, and child abuse. Sexually transmitted diseases are now common among the monied professional classes, not just the underclass. The poor are encouraged by state legislatures to squander their hard-earned dollars (or welfare checks) on state-run lotteries and numbers games. A suicide doctor and his lawyers persuade successive juries that for depressed terminally ill patients, execution is as desirable a treatment as hospice care, and carbon monoxide a medically acceptable agent for the relief of pain.

In the nation's high schools, teachers less competent than their predecessors create a generation of graduates less competent than *their* predecessors, while outside their classrooms security guards and police officers monitor the halls. Small wonder that for years now, students have been arriving on university campuses with lower test scores than the entering freshmen of previous generations. Before they graduate, many students are led to believe that the university's proper role is to be not so much an arena for study and reflection as a cockpit for power struggles over gender and ethnicity. On many campuses, the literary and historic canon once accepted as the source of civilized and humane learning is now derided as a corrupt device for perpetuating the hegemony of oppressive European males.

America's religious life is equally chaotic. A recent poll pegged the proportion of Americans describing themselves as regular churchgoers at its lowest level in memory: 37 percent. Once flourishing mainline religious denominations flirt with apostasy, hemorrhage members, and collapse toward bankruptcy, while cults, covens, and New Age mumbo-jumbo thrive. Media coverage of religion seems to oscillate between stories of controversy (abortion, school prayer, the ordination of homosexuals) and stories of corruption (Catholic clergymen molesting altar boys; Protestant evangelists fleecing their contributors, patronizing prostitutes, or both). In a bookstore not long ago, I saw a sign above a display that seemed to sum up the nation's spiritual confusion: "Psychology, Religion and the Occult."

Should orthodox Christians despair? Not at all. The Apostle Paul faced a situation arguably as bad.

It is my purpose in this chapter to put forward three arguments:

- First, American culture is in decline and chaos because it has become unmoored from two noble traditions, one religious, one secular.
- Second, many Christian churches, and many individual Christians, are responding to this cultural decline and chaos in disastrously ham-handed ways.

- Third, the situation presents an exciting opportunity for Christians to do their work on earth more gently, shrewdly, and effectively.

The Culture of Chaos

The defining characteristic of our culture is chaos. There are few agreed-upon rules of moral, aesthetic, or civic conduct, and the existing rules are often the subject of angry, unresolved debate. Amid this chaos, perhaps the most universally accepted rule is that every individual has the right to devise his or her own rules, and that one person's self-devised standards are as good as another's. The cheerleaders for such radical personal autonomy, of course, do not acknowledge that it produces anarchy or chaos; they prefer terms like "freedom" or "pluralism."

Their forebears who launched the American experiment in democracy, however, would surely find the notion of unfettered personal freedom and self-invented rules uncongenial; the Founders in their day deplored the unrestrained license of the mob. They celebrated self-restraint, and warned that individual liberty must be tempered with republican *virtue*—a word whose present meaning denotes moral purity, but whose ancient Latin root suggests strength and competence.

Our contemporary culture of chaos and moral relativism, then, which increasingly we accept as normal, is *not* normal, if we reach back in history to compare. Today's culture of chaos is a twentieth-century phenomenon, linked to a collective loss of faith in transcendent values and to our resulting loss of a common moral vocabulary.

When we read the essays and speeches of our eighteenth- and nineteenth-century forebears, one of the most striking revelations is the extent to which they shared a common moral vocabulary. For all their lively debates and disagreements, the Founders' public lives and discussions were conducted in the context of a shared moral culture to which virtually all gave assent. If we imagine culture to be a river in which everyone swims, or from which everybody drinks, the culture of our forebears was created out of two great tributaries: the Judeo-Christian biblical tradition and the Greco-Roman classical tradition.

Thomas Jefferson, for example, was not conventionally religious: "I am a cult unto myself," he wrote. Yet Jefferson clearly believed in a Creator—an "Author of Liberty"—and he pored over the New Testament in an effort to devise an ethical system based solely on Jesus' actual words. Benjamin Franklin likewise was not conventionally religious. Yet he, too, was knowledgeable about biblical religion and friendly to it, and his writings are replete with biblical references. Franklin spoke without embarrassment of the infant United States as "the new Israel," for example.

References by our political forebears to the classical tradition are equally commonplace; America was also called "the new Athens." And what is striking to the modern reader is not only that our early leaders were steeped in biblical and classical lore: They were, after all, members of an educated elite. What is remarkable is that these leaders assumed a similar knowledge of these two great traditions among the plainer people to whom they spoke.

Both of the principal speakers at the dedication of the Gettysburg cemetery, Abraham Lincoln and the scholar-diplomat Edward Everett, drew from the two great tributaries in their remarks. And both appear to have been totally confident that their audiences— the immediate audience at the dedication and, later, the reading audience—had also drunk from the same double stream.

As Gary Wills suggests in his richly fascinating book of 1992, *Lincoln at Gettysburg,* Lincoln could be certain that when he used the phrase "a new birth of Freedom," his words would resonate deeply with a populace who knew by heart the language of spiritual rebirth in the Gospel of John. His Gettysburg Address was also patterned, Wills writes, upon the classical form for funeral orations laid down by the ancient Greeks. Lincoln, railsplitter and backwoodsman though he may have been, was familiar with the rhetoric of Pericles.

Everett also filled his two-hour oration at Gettysburg with rhetoric gleaned from both great tributaries. He used cadences derived from the King James Bible, and direct biblical language, quoting the prophet Amos and the Apostle Paul. He evoked scenes from ancient Greece, comparing the dead at Gettysburg to the Athenian heroes of the Battle of Marathon, as if he expected his listeners to know exactly what he was talking about.

I emphasize the importance of these two traditions to an earlier America in order to arrive at a crucial point: Both traditions, the religious and the secular, had an important feature in common. Each accepted the notion of objective, even absolute, values; each asserted the reality of something called Truth, with a capital "T." The religious tradition asserted that the God of Moses was the source of ultimate authority; this tradition arrived at objective values and Truth through the instrumentality of divine revelation. But the Greeks also believed in objective truths and absolutes; the dialogues of Plato show Socrates and his protégés searching for the *summum bonum* and for objective ideals of justice, beauty, and truth, discernible through reason and rational discourse.

The two tributaries of Western tradition, in short, gave our forebears a common moral culture and a common moral vocabulary: a culture that generally accepted the notion of transcendent truths and values; truths that existed whether or not mortals chose to acknowledge them; rules that had authority, whether or not mortals chose to obey them. Even the moderate and pragmatic Aristotle derived a set of coherent rules of aesthetics and politics that he believed to be objective, not self-invented.

Today's culture and today's style of angry but inconclusive moral and political discourse, exist, by contrast, with little or no reference to these two great traditions. Indeed, today's lack of moral consensus—today's culture of moral relativism and near-worship of the uninhibited, unfettered Self—suggests that twentieth-century America has been drinking from some other cultural stream than the river formed by the biblical and classical tributaries.

Dr. Gene Edward Veith Jr. has suggested what that other source may be. In a thoughtful and disturbing book, *Modern Fascism: Liquidating the Judeo-Christian Worldview,* he puts forward the idea that the secular culture of modern America can be traced to dark and turbid headwaters that start with the nihilists and Nietzsche and course through Heidegger and the European existentialists.

This stream of thought, Dr. Veith reminds us, has as one of its objects the total overthrow of both the classical tradition and the

Judeo-Christian heritage. It was Nietzsche, for example, who proclaimed dramatically that since religion is a mere projection of human wishes, "God is dead." It was Nietzsche who denounced both Judaism and Christianity as "slave religions." And it was Nietzsche who advanced a new version of the *summum bonum*: an Aryan ideal of "race, of breeding, of privilege," whose chief exemplar would be a New Man—a Superman—who would be "capable of creating pain and suffering, and must experience pleasure in so doing."

Modern scholars, Dr. Veith notes, tend to underestimate Nietzsche as a sort of operatic prose stylist, forgetting that his thought attracted serious adherents and had real consequences. The celebrated existentialist Martin Heidegger, for example, expanded on the idea of the death of God in his rectoral address at Freiburg University: "If God is dead," he said approvingly, "there is no longer a transcendental authority or reference point for objective truth. . . . [T]o make one's own rules is the highest freedom."

Heidegger became a Nazi—one so radical that his Nazi superiors finally parted company with him over his desire to persecute Catholic students at Freiburg. And Heidegger, like his fellow European existentialists, seized upon the idea of self-invented values as liberating. For them, rebellion—against the classical tradition and against Judeo-Christian religious tenets—was a creative act. They celebrated the immanent, the earthly and immediate, deriding older notions of transcendent norms and objective values.

Such ideas have had far-reaching consequences. Ten years after the end of World War II Walter Lippmann complained, in his *Essays in the Public Philosophy,* that although the Western democracies had triumphed militarily in that great conflict, they may have been defeated spiritually and morally. Certain alien ideas had crept into Western life and thought, Lippmann observed—ideas that caused postwar civilization in the industrial democracies to be philosophically and politically "deranged." Lippmann, himself not at all religious, nevertheless deplored the West's modern loss of faith in transcendent values, the loss of what he fondly called "the mandate of Heaven."

"If what is good, what is right, what is true, is only what the individual 'chooses' to 'invent,'" he wrote, "then we are outside the tradition of civility. We are back in the war of all . . . against all." Lippmann traced the derangement of traditional values to a new philosophy that was emphatically not drawn from the two great tributaries of Western thought—a malign new philosophy that argued the primacy of the human will, that gloried in power, that found glamour in violence. Such notions, he wrote in 1955, eroded the notion of citizenship, sapped the power of leaders to govern, and made civilization dysfunctional.

Writing in the relatively calm air of the 1950s, Lippmann defined the twin tributaries—Judeo-Christian thought and the classical tradition, reaching down through the Enlightenment—as part of America's essential "public philosophy." Without a firm grip on that shared public philosophy, he wrote, civility, and perhaps even civilization, would die away. "The crucial point," he wrote, "is not whether naturalists and supernaturalists disagree. . . . It is that they [should] agree that there is a valid Law which, whether it [is derived from] the commandment of God or the reason of things, [is] transcendent[:] not someone's fantasy, wish or rationalization, but there objectively. . . . It can be discovered. It [has] to be obeyed."

The Political Temptation

Is America unwittingly fascist, as Dr. Veith avers? Or merely "deranged," in Lippmann's melancholy view? One need not agree totally with either author about the sources or degree of our moral and spiritual dysfunction to acknowledge that today's cult of the imperial, autonomous Self has been disastrous in social terms. Unmoored from ancient traditions, "liberated" from fidelity to the idea of objective truth, our modern culture of chaos values self-expression above self-discipline. The rise of moral relativism and enthusiasm for self-invented rules has produced, as Lippmann predicted, a culture of chaos and perpetual contention, recalling indeed the specter of Hobbes' "war of all against all."

How should Christian churches (and individual Christians) respond to this cultural challenge? Christian faith, of course, is first and foremost about the well-being of immortal souls, about the relationship of individual souls to an eternal God: "A charge to keep I have; a God to glorify; a never-dying soul to save, and fit it for the sky." But Christians should not shrink from the reality that their tradition is also a cultural treasure for this world, and that "this world" is the arena given by God to Christians for acting out their faith. Charles Wesley's great hymn quite properly turns, in its second verse, to that temporal arena: "To serve the present age, my calling to fulfill; O may it all my powers engage, To do my Master's will."

It is a sad irony, however, that a time of maximum need for the redemptive work of the church in this world has too often found churches stumbling toward precisely the wrong solutions.

America's mainline Protestant churches, for example, have suffered their greatest decline in members, contributions, influence, and effectiveness during precisely the same years that they have struggled most avidly for political and cultural power. For years, the denominations once accurately described as "mainline" have selected their agendas almost totally from the steam-table of hot issues in the secular political culture: Nuclear disarmament. The nuclear freeze. Women's rights. Gay rights. Farmers' rights. Workers' rights. The Cold War. Universal health insurance. "Empowerment" of the poor and dispossessed. Various *soi-disant* liberation movements at home and abroad.

Desperately eager to be seen as "prophetic," wistfully desiring to be "relevant," mainline church professionals over three decades have beckoned their flocks willy-nilly to the partisan political barricades and pell-mell into corporate disaster. A nadir of sorts was reached when mainline social-witness activists marched hopefully to Central America in the 1980s, in support of revolutionary movements later proved to be so violent, coercive, and corrupt that even the most earnest defenders of social-witness politics were shocked into embarrassed silence.

The self-destruction of the mainline churches by succumbing to the political temptation over the past thirty years, however, is apparently not a sufficient cautionary example to evangelical churches. As if in imitation, their clergy and professionals are marching to the right-wing barricades today as eagerly as their mainline siblings marched to the left-wing ramparts: joining "Christian" coalitions,

Transmogrify = To change in appearance or form

mog'ra fī

manning phone banks, endorsing candidates, and advocating specific legislative remedies with the same naive fervor that brought their mainline brethren first to distraction from their true mission, then to irrelevance and near-ruin.

Christian theonomists and Christian reconstructionists are seeking to establish, through coercive legal and political means, a political simulacrum of the kingdom of God, as surely as mainline "fraternal workers" sought to establish their version of that kingdom arm in arm with the Sandinista Party. In the process, they abandon the eternal for the evanescent, exactly as their mainline counterparts have done; they distract themselves and their flocks from the legitimate mission of the church in this world; and they bid—unwittingly, perhaps, but blasphemously nonetheless—to substitute political coercion for the free working of God's grace.

Can anyone doubt that the evangelical dalliance with the political temptation will be fully as disillusioning and damaging as the mainline's similar flirtation? Three wise maxims should be posted on the walls of every evangelical church—or tattooed, perhaps, on every evangelical forearm—as warnings against succumbing to the political temptation. The first is from the New Testament: "Put not your faith in princes." The second is from Martin Luther: "I would rather be governed by a wise Turk than a stupid Christian." The third is from the winsome and incomparable C. S. Lewis: "Jesus tells us to feed the hungry, but He does not give cooking lessons."

Ministering in the Culture of Chaos

If marching to the political barricades is the wrong mission for the church in this world, what is the right mission? What, precisely, should be the cultural mission of the church?

Let me suggest three answers to this question.

The first answer is deceptively simple-sounding. It is that the church's task in this world is to be the church.

I say "deceptively simple-sounding" because the temptation is so great for the church to transmogrify itself into something else: today a Broadway theater, tomorrow a protest movement; next Saturday, *tmg ni clements*

Task

a social club or singles bar, the next day a political party decked out in choir robes and priestly vestments.

The tasks of the church are worship, education, the equipping of the saints, pastoral care, and evangelism. If churches allow themselves to fail at these tasks, success at other, lesser tasks will mean nothing. If they hold faithfully to these tasks, on the other hand, nothing can hold them back, and their redemptive influence on the culture will be mighty indeed.

The long collapse of the mainline churches into confusion and irrelevance, remember, took place in tiny increments: this amateurish symposium on health care costs piled atop that muddled debate about nuclear deterrence; this divisive, half-informed squabble about the regime in North Korea added to that earnest, chin-rubbing denominational study of labor policy in East Anglia. Every hour wasted upon such distractions was an opportunity lost—an opportunity lost to steep Christians in the essential lore—the powerfully transforming lore!—of their faith and their tradition. Over time, confusion about mission led to more serious complications: biblical illiteracy and spiritual ennui. People become malnourished in two ways: by eating too little, and by eating too much of the wrong things.

A second task (and opportunity) for the church in this world is to redouble its efforts in education, especially higher education.

The "equipping of the saints" is not just a task for the Sunday school classroom. America's small liberal arts colleges, many of them denominational institutions, have for nearly two centuries had a favorable impact on the culture out of all proportion to their size and wealth. A nation suffering an intellectual and moral crisis needs more such institutions now, and better ones.

CS Lewis

C. S. Lewis was right: Jesus does not offer cooking lessons—there is, in other words, no such thing as "Christian cuisine," and no such thing as "Christian politics" or "Christian engineering." But Lewis must have known a Christian cook or two, and surely it is possible to train Christian politicians, Christian physicians, Christian filmmakers, Christian journalists, and Christian engineers. Not "Christians" trained to be narrow, sectarian, and piously intolerant in the mode of the church lady of "Saturday Night Live" fame, but educated Christians who are humane, broadly cultured, formidably competent, and self-assured about the contributions they can make to a lost and hungry world. Producing such leaders is the exciting challenge facing a new generation of church-linked colleges and universities.

Those colleges and universities must be the sites where the biblical and classical traditions are recovered, rehabilitated, joined to one another, and proudly taught again.

Those Christian institutions of higher learning, incidentally, will do well not to do battle with science and the scientific way of knowing. Their ambition, instead, should be to persuade science and scientists not to be arrogant: not to imagine that science, which is a valid and useful tool for understanding the material world, has anything at all to tell us about the immaterial world. The hopeful task for Christian professors in Christian colleges is not to defeat science; it is to score a victory for other valid ways of knowing that science arrogantly ignores, marginalizes, or rejects—the aesthetic way of knowing, for example, and, importantly, the religious way of knowing. The religious way of knowing, after all, has been accepted and employed by such intellectuals as John Milton, John Donne, John Calvin, and Gerard Manley Hopkins, and has given the world the Sistine Madonna of Raphael, the *Divine Comedy* of Dante, the *St. Matthew Passion* of Bach, and the poems of Gerard Manley Hopkins.

A third task for the living church in a dying culture is to communicate an important truth to faithful Christians: that "spiritual warfare" must not be the same as actual warfare.

The biblical admonition that we Christians should put on the breastplate of righteousness and gird up our loins with truth is important, but clearly metaphorical. And the operative word in the opening line of that beloved old hymn about Christian soldiers is that we should march *as* to war, not actually *to* it.

Why is this an important point? Because too often today Christians are adding to the angry combativeness that is a lamentable mark of our chaotic contemporary culture.

It is true that the provocations to Christians from that culture are serious and reprehensible. In particular, Christians who describe themselves as orthodox or evangelical find themselves contending these days against a hostile, even aggressively hostile culture. And surely, facing that culture of aggressive unbelief, Christians have a duty to persevere—to live lives of persistent, unrelenting assertion.

The style and tone of that assertion, however, must be wisely and carefully calibrated to comport strictly with the commandment of love that is the first rule for Christians. Muscular Christians who love the rough and tumble of spiritual warfare will instantly retort, correctly, that true Christian love must have high standards and be demanding, like the love of a good father; that true Christian love must have nothing resembling that flabby, anything-goes tolerance that pretends to be love, but is actually mere indifference. They deserve a response, and it is this: Even the demanding love of a father is still recognizable as love; it is not so strident, censorious, arrogant, and angry that it resembles something called hate.

What specific lessons might churches and Christian leaders teach believers about the right way to contend with that hostile, unbelieving culture?

One, surely, is that human freedom is central to the gospel; that the gospel recognizes and accepts a degree of human freedom that will lead some humans to wreak tragedy and ruin upon themselves and others. In one of Jesus' parables he describes the propagation of the kingdom of God as resembling a sower casting seed. Not all of that seed finds a fertile place to grow, Jesus reminds us; some seed, inevitably, falls on rocky ground. Jesus is warning us, is he not, that access to God's grace can only come through free choice. He is warning us, moreover, that not every free person will make the right choice. Christians should grieve over every soul who refuses to make a saving choice, as Jesus wept over Jerusalem. But we must never imagine that we can coerce such choices or find political and legal shortcuts to the kingdom of God.

Another lesson about how to respond to a hostile and anarchic culture can be found in the rich language of family love that permeates the Scriptures. In our own families, do we not find ourselves contending with brothers or daughters or sons who refuse to bend to our beliefs and our ways? If we are wise Christians, we do not expel them from the circle of our love: We pray for these prodigal children; we exhort them, and we love them, with a demanding and sometimes impatient love (as indeed we should love our prodigal, disobedient selves). Should it be any different with a prodigal world—a world over which we are given "dominion," which suggests fatherly affection?

A final lesson to temper us as we confront a culture that is increasingly hostile to Christian faith is the reality that God truly holds sovereign and ultimate power over the universe. Given the state of contemporary culture, it is tempting to become discouraged. Too much discouragement, however—too much rage at the world's waywardness—may be a symptom of overweening dependence upon ourselves and our human powers. Do we truly believe that God is the King and Sovereign of the universe?

There are three tasks, then, for the church and its people in a fallen, failing, and hostile culture:

- First, the evangelical church must hold to its historic priorities of worship, teaching, pastoral care, and evangelism—and not imagine that political shortcuts can further the work of the kingdom. To renounce such shortcuts will not diminish the power of the church to do good in the world; it will enhance it.

- Second, the evangelical church must become a force in education, especially higher education—a force determined to reclaim and reassert the intellectual traditions, biblical and classical, which are the basis for true civilization. To do so will seed the world with individual Christian leaders, strikingly competent in their fields, who will act out the drama of "overcoming evil with good."

- Third, the evangelical church must teach its people the true arts of spiritual war, whose weapons are the persuasive power of superior ideas coupled with a gentle, unrelenting love. Those who teach and learn this lesson will discover the true excitement of Jesus' admonition to be "wise as serpents and gentle as doves," or of C. S. Lewis' observation that the true Christian is like a secret agent, parachuted by God behind enemy lines.

A Role Model

I said at the outset that the Apostle Paul almost certainly faced a culture as wayward and difficult as our own. That fact should surely give heart to any Christian weeping over the secular city of today.

Paul faced, first of all, a new and largely unformed church, riven with disputes between the Judaizers, who wished to impose old Hebraic rules, and the Hellenizers, whose message was more universal and whose understanding of human freedom was certainly more profound. Paul faced a world with no agreed-upon scriptural canon to rely upon or even to argue about. He confronted a world which, like ours, worshiped many gods—but one, moreover, in which monotheism, the powerful idea of One True God, had nothing of the reach and power it has attained today. Paul faced conditions of moral and sexual libertinism at least as troubling as those of today—and they stared at him not just from within the general culture, but from within the church at Corinth.

If it is possible for Christians to follow Jesus, then surely we can follow Paul. And if Paul could succeed in setting in motion the transformation of a culture, then surely we face an exciting project, and one with at least some possibility of progress and success.

We are calling the church,

amidst our dying culture,

to repent of its worldliness,

to recover and confess the truth of

God's Word

as did the Reformers,

and to see that truth embodied

in doctrine, worship, and life.

3

Contending for Truth
in an Age of Anti-Truth

R. Albert Mohler Jr.

n the context of modern Western civilization and in areas increasingly permeated by Western culture, it is not easy to retain and live within the theistic framework presupposed and taught by all the Christian churches."[1] Thus reflected Professor Brian Hebblethwaite, Lecturer in Divinity at Cambridge University and Canon Theologian of Leicester Cathedral.

Hebblethwaite's lament did not erupt in a vacuum. To the contrary, he was responding with vigor to his Cambridge colleague, Don Cupitt, the so-called atheist priest.[2] Some years earlier, Cupitt had "taken leave of God," and yet continued as a priest in the Church of England.[3] Beyond this, in 1984 the British Broadcast Corporation had produced and broadcast a major series entitled "The Sea of Faith," featuring Cupitt and his radically interiorized and heretical notions of truth and Christianity. It was to this series and the accompanying book that Hebblethwaite responded. Christianity is not about a sea of faith, he asserted, but about an ocean of truth.

The literary and theological encounter between Cupitt and Hebblethwaite is remarkable, not because two Cambridge theologians were engaged in a highly publicized debate, but because their unlikely debate is so illustrative of the great divide in Western culture and, tragically, in the Christian churches.

The modern world is at war with the very notion of truth. The mixed legacy of the Enlightenment has devolved into the pernicious and pervasive influence of a culture committed to anti-truth. The conservative influence of the Scottish Enlightenment, which gave rise to the American experiment of ordered liberty, has been eclipsed by the anomie and moral anarchy of the continental Enlightenment. In our century, well described by historian Eric Hobsbawm as "the age of extremes,"[4] "Goddess Reason," once worshiped in revolutionary Paris, has given way to the idols of irrationality.

The contours of the modern secular worldview are apparent in the discourse and drama of everyday life. The scientific worldview of naturalism supplanted the notion of Creator and creation; the rise of critical philosophies assaulted revelation and inspiration; the ascendancy of humanism swept away thoughts of sin and limitation; the hubris of the age cast aside providence and the divine government; the emergence of the imperial self rejected all fear of judgment and divine wrath. Skepticism has given way to atheism, rationalism has lapsed into irrationality, pluralism has given way to relativism.

Modernity's Assault on Truth

In its modern phase, Western culture sought to dominate truth, to wrest authority from the church and bring truth under its mechanistic and rationalized control, just as the engines of technology had gained control over the forces of nature. But in its present phase, Western culture has moved to reject the very notion of truth and to embrace relativism, nihilism, and radical subjectivism.

Modernity has given way to postmodernity, which is simply modernity in its latest guise. Claiming that all notions of truth are socially constructed, the postmodernists are committed to total war on truth itself, a deconstructionist project bent on the casting down of all religious, philosophical, political, and cultural authorities.[5] A postmodernist ahead of his times, Karl Marx warned that in the light of modernity, "all that is solid melts into air." It is precisely to this mission of vaporization that the deconstructionists are committed.

In the wake of this project of deconstruction is left the debris of truth and virtue, order and structure, orthodoxy and heresy. As postmodern critic Matei Calinescu comments,

> Even more difficult to defend in a pluralistic age like ours is the idea of an orthodoxy by whose standards we could decide whether this or that tendency is heretical or not. Our specific time consciousness, which has brought about the loss of transcendence, is also responsible for the present-day conceptual emptiness of the opposition between orthodoxy and heresy.[6]

All this would be tragic enough if such trends shaped the consciousness of the world, but not of the church. Yet to our shame, the modern secular worldview has wrought destruction within the church as well. The modern attempt to dominate truth has given way within sectors of the church to the postmodern rejection of truth itself. Indeed, in many denominations and churches, notions of orthodoxy and heresy have become "conceptual emptiness." The boundaries have vanished.[7] The very possibility of heresy is dismissed in many circles within mainline Protestantism, and many evangelicals seem to have no better grasp of the moral imperative to honor the truth and to oppose error.[8] Matters of truth and falsehood are not matters of moral indifference to the Christian church. We are to contend for the faith, and the love of the truth is an essential mark of the believer.[9] An attitude of indifference, whether based in postmodern deconstructionist theory or simple epistemological apathy, is a scandal to the gospel and a looming threat to the church.

Confessing Christians love the truth and refute error, not in a spirit of pride and vindictiveness, but in a spirit of humility and faithfulness. Our responsibility is clear, as articulated well by Blaise Pascal:

> It is as much a crime to disturb the peace when truth prevails as it is to keep the peace when truth is violated. There is therefore a time in which peace is justified and another time when it is not justifiable. For it is written that there is a time for peace and a time for war and it is the law of truth that distinguishes the two. But at no time is there a time for truth and a time for error, for it is written that God's truth shall abide forever. That is why Christ has said that He has come to bring peace and at the same time that He has come to bring the sword. But He does not say that He has come to bring both the truth and falsehood.[10]

The secularization of mainline Protestantism and the dominant theological academy is evident in the evisceration of the Christian truth-claim at the hands of the theologians and church leadership. Virtually no doctrinal essential has been left untouched, no truth left intact, no creed or confession defended against compromise. Increasingly—in the name of pluralism, tolerance, inclusivity, and sensitivity—all that is solid appears indeed to melt into air.

And yet the tragedy is not limited to mainline liberal Protestantism. The modern secular worldview is increasingly apparent within evangelicalism as well. An aversion to doctrinal Christianity has been growing for several decades, along with an increasing intolerance for doctrinal and confessional accountability. Evangelicals have embraced the technologies of modernity, often without recognizing that these technologies have claimed the role of master rather than servant.

The ubiquitous culture of consumerism and materialism has seduced many evangelicals into a ministry mode driven by marketing rather than mission. To an ever greater extent, evangelicals are accommodating themselves to moral compromise in the name of lifestyle and choice. Authentic biblical worship is often supplanted by the entertainment culture as issues of performance and taste displace the simplicity and God-centeredness of true worship.

Voices within and without warn of a crisis of truth among evangelicals. Theologian David Wells argues that modernity has left virtually "no place for truth."[11] Sociologists have traced the increasingly secular message of evangelical preaching and the triumph of the autonomous self over theological concerns in evangelical piety.[12] James Davison Hunter has traced and projected the pattern of "cognitive bargaining" by which the younger generation of evangelical intellectuals is increasingly forfeiting biblical orthodoxy in the face of academic hostility.[13] A candid survey reveals even more ominous signs. Some evangelicals are embracing the radical subjectivity, perspectivalism, dehistoricism, and relativism of the postmodernist academy. In the name of a paradigm shift, the claim to objective truth has itself been forfeited by some evangelicals. Book and chapter titles such as *Truth Is Stranger Than It Used to Be* and "There's No Such Thing as Objective Truth and It's a Good Thing, Too" serve notice that postmodernism is not merely a problem external to evangelicalism.[14]

Indeed, evidence of the embrace of relativistic, subjectivistic, perspectival, privatistic, and constructivist theories of truth is widespread among evangelicals. In the name of narrative some have discarded propositions, and are thus unable or unwilling to make any statement of propositional truth. In the name of pluralism some have excluded the existence of absolute truth, and have thus abdicated the foundation of Christian truth, only to land in various relativisms. In the name of perspectivalism, some have rejected the unity of truth and embraced unconditional subjectivity. In order to gain distance from "foundationalism," many evangelicals have abandoned the foundation.

The Postmodern Evangelicals

Indeed, the problem is remarkably evident among those who identify themselves as "postmodern evangelicals." Stanley Grenz of Carey Theological College and Regent College declares that nothing less than a new intellectual era has dawned. Grenz asserts that the church should "claim the new postmodern context for Christ" and establish new paradigms for expressing the faith.[15] An appropriate postmodern evangelicalism, suggests Grenz, would recognize a "post-fundamentalist shift" that establishes the new evangelical landscape. Evangelicals must shift from a "creed-based" paradigm to a "spirituality based" model of faith and theology. The old propositional paradigm must be set aside as a relic of a long gone, seldom lamented evangelical past. As Grenz argues, "Evangelical theologians ought to move away from conceiving their task as merely to discover divinely disclosed truth understood as the single, unified doctrinal system purportedly lodged within the pages of the Bible and waiting to be categorized and systematized."[16]

Thus, evangelicals should reject their claim to propositional truth because the postmodern age no longer respects the notion of objective, absolute, or revealed truth. Propositions are bothersome, precisely because they force the issue of truth and falsehood. Given this fact, and the nearly universal rejection of propositional theology in the modern age, evangelicals should, according to Grenz, revision evangelical theology as a "practical discipline" serving the believing community, rather than as a discipline that would order itself by the restatement of propositions.

What about the Bible? If propositional approaches are off limits, how are we to speak of the nature and authority of Scripture? Grenz suggests that the Bible is indeed authoritative, but only because the community of faith has granted it this status. For the church, the Bible is "the book of the community," and thus bears appropriate authority within the community.

This approach, which might be characterized as authority "from below" rather than "from above," is suggested in the term "post-foundationalism." Consistent with post-foundationalism, the community of interpretation becomes the locus of authority, for, even where this is denied, the community stands over the Word. Authority and meaning, as well as the Bible and the notion of truth itself, are all seen as extensions of the community, rather than as a revelation addressed to the community.

Behind the postmodern evangelicals stands a constellation of academic figures and movements. Influential among these is the so-called New Yale Theology associated with theologians such as George Lindbeck, Hans Frei, Paul Holmer, and David Kelsey.[17] Behind the New Yale Theology stands the influence of anthropologist Clifford Geertz, who suggests that all meaning is community-based and expressed through "cultural-linguistic systems." Also behind the movement stands Ludwig Wittgenstein, whose notion of truth as "language games" is inherently and inevitably corrosive of what Francis Schaeffer was candid to call "true truth."

The issue of objective truth was raised anew by William H. Willimon of Duke University in the pages of *Christianity Today*.[18] Evangelicals who attempt to defend the reality and knowability of objective truth are, asserts Willimon, "making a tactical mistake." "Jesus did not," Willimon states, "arrive among us enunciating a set of propositions that we are to affirm."[19] Instead, Willimon suggests, Jesus came declaring himself and inviting persons to follow him. According to Willimon, Jesus did not insist that persons believe propositions about himself, which we might characterize as objective truth.

We are not left to utter subjectively, Willimon insists, because "the truth of Jesus is utterly inseparable from him—his life, death, and resurrection."[20] Here we are left with only two options: Either Willimon sees no objective reality to the life, death, and resurrection of Jesus, or he has just violated his own injunction. We will hope for the latter.

When persons invoke "truth," Willimon argues, "what they usually really mean is that they have some preconception of what truth is, and they have heard some assertion that matches their preconception."[21] In bare form, this is the constructivist notion of truth masquerading as missiology. Willimon is certainly correct in insisting that the gospel calls for far more than mere intellectual assent. But we must insist that the gospel does require intellectual assent.

Willimon has created a straw-man argument, suggesting that some evangelicals conceive conversion as mere intellectual assent to objective truths. I have never met an evangelical who would make such an argument. Forfeiting a claim to objective truth may be academically convenient in a postmodern age, but it spells disaster for the church.

If the postmodern evangelicals have their way, how would evangelicalism differ from its founding form? Stanley Grenz suggests that we should see a shift from a "creed-based" evangelicalism to a "spirituality based" postmodern evangelicalism. As he states, "In recent years we have begun to shift the focus of our attention away from doctrine, with its focus on propositional truth in favor of a renewed interest in what constitutes the uniquely evangelical vision of spirituality."[22]

This is a false and dangerous dichotomy. Those who set the creeds against spirituality have set themselves against the spirituality represented by the creeds. As J. Gresham Machen argued:

> The creeds of Christendom are not expressions of Christian experience. They are summary statements of what God has told us in his Word. Far from the subject matter of the creeds being derived from Christian experience, it is Christian experience which is based upon the truth contained in the creeds; and the truth contained in the creeds is derived from the Bible, which is the Word of God.[23]

Grenz would liberate evangelicalism from propositional truth so that "a uniquely evangelical vision of spirituality may flourish." But without doctrine, without propositional truth, without the truth of God's Word, the vision of spirituality may indeed be unique but it cannot be evangelical.

These false dichotomies are at the heart of evangelical postmodernism. Propositional truth is set against spirituality; objective truth is pitted against the call to discipleship; and doctrine is set against devotion—all in the name of postmodernism.

The further dissolution of the evangelical academy is evident in *Truth Is Stranger Than It Used to Be* by J. Richard Middleton and Brian J. Walsh of Toronto's Institute for Christian Studies.[24] Middleton and Walsh present a portrait of postmodernism on the advance, destroying all "metanarratives" and rejecting the totalizing, oppressive, patriarchalist, and hegemonistic character of objective truth-claims.

We must adapt Christianity to this new reality, they argue. The reality of their own agenda is clear when the authors address the nature and authority of Scripture. Identifying some texts as oppressive "texts of terror," Walsh and Middleton would set the text of the Bible against itself, applying an internal critique to Scripture. In the course of this critique, of course, some biblical texts must be rejected as true and normative. As Middleton and Walsh argue, "the traditional approach of claiming that since the Bible is the Word of God we should simply swallow our objections and submit to the text's authority" is to be gladly discarded.[25]

Walsh and Middleton are not alone in pressing for a postmodern evangelical paradigm. Philip D. Kenneson makes his argument transparent in his essay, "There's No Such Thing as Objective Truth, and It's a Good Thing, Too."[26] Kenneson throws out not only the reality of objective truth, but also the notion of the correspondence of truth and objective reality. Christians should not, he argues, answer the "truth question" at all. As he insists, "the sooner we see that we needn't, the sooner we can get on with the business of being Christians, which in no way entails accepting a certain philosophical account of truth, justification, and 'reality.'"[27]

The implications of this statement are shattering. Kenneson straightforwardly argues that we should get over the truth question so that we can get on with being Christians. This has been tried before, and we have rightly called it heresy. Where there is no claim to truth, there is no Christianity. Those who argue for this kind of postmodern evangelical paradigm, if consistent with their own epistemological principles, cannot even articulate what Christianity is, or why Jesus came, or what he accomplished.

Unnoticed by the evangelical mainstream, now focused on largely pragmatic and therapeutic concerns, these postmodern evangelicals are redefining the very nature of truth, the gospel, the Bible, and the evangelical tradition. Their influence is extensive and growing, and younger evangelicals often hear the postmodernist arguments without any rebuttal. The reach of the postmodernist proposals is seen in the fact that these arguments are made in the pages of *Christianity Today* and in books published by InterVarsity Press.

While we must name and oppose the relativisms that mark our age, we should also recognize that relativistic positions never hold. Relativism inevitably slides into nihilism. Standing behind these postmodern proposals are not merely the New Yale theologians, Clifford Geertz, or even Wittgenstein—it is Nietzsche. The acids of modernity burn down to the vapors of nihilism. The ambiguities of pervasive relativisms are too much for us to bear, and relativism becomes nihilism. Now, nihilism is present even within the evangelical academy.

A careful consideration of the evangelical movement is in order. Evangelicalism can be considered as a multistoried building. On the upper floors evangelical theologians debate doctrinal issues, and rightly so. We must contend for substitutionary atonement, Chalcedonian Christology, forensic justification, and justification by grace alone, through faith alone, in Christ alone—and for other evangelical essentials. But, at the same time, we must recognize that on the first floor the doctrine of revelation is under attack, and the issue of biblical inerrancy remains assaulted. If the solid rock of biblical authority and total truthfulness is forfeited, the arguments taking place on the upper stories are certain to be lost. Yet even this is not the base of the problem, for beneath the foundation, some are attacking the very notion of truth itself. Some of those contending on the first floor for the inerrancy of the Bible are unaware that threats to evangelical integrity and faithfulness are present even beneath their feet. In some evangelical circles, it is almost impossible to discuss, debate, or defend the doctrine of biblical inerrancy, for the very notion of truth has been abandoned. The entire debate has become nonsensical.

Compromise and Confusion in the Churches

The problem of postmodern evangelicalism is not limited to the evangelical academy. Researchers increasingly report that a majority of evangelicals reject the notion of absolute or objective truth. The seductive lure of postmodern relativism has pervaded many evangelical pulpits and countless evangelical pews, often couched as humility, sensitivity, or sophistication. The culture has us in its grip, and many feel no discomfort.

The absence of doctrinal precision and biblical preaching marks the current evangelical age. Doctrine is considered outdated by some and divisive by others. The confessional heritage of the church is neglected and, in some cases, seems even to be an embarrassment to updated evangelicals. Expository preaching—once the hallmark and distinction of the evangelical pulpit—has been replaced in many churches by motivational messages, therapeutic massaging of the self, and formulas for health, prosperity, personal integration, and celestial harmony.

Almost a century ago, J. C. Ryle, the great evangelical bishop, warned of such diversions from truth:

> I am afraid of an inward disease which appears to be growing and spreading in all the Churches of Christ throughout the world. That

disease is a disposition on the part of ministers to abstain from all sharply-cut doctrine, and a distaste on the part of professing Christians for all distinct statements of dogmatic truth.[28]

A century later, Ryle's diagnosis is seen as prophetic, and the disease is assuredly terminal. The various strains of the truth-relativizing virus are indicated by different symptoms and diverse signs, but the end is the same. Among the strains now threatening the evangelical churches is the temptation to find a halfway house between modernity and biblical truth.[29] Another is the call for an "evangelical mega-shift," which would transform orthodox evangelical conviction into the categories of modern process thought.[30] This is a road that leads to disaster and away from the faith once for all delivered to the saints.

Thus, the church finds itself assaulted without—and even within—by a culture and worldview of untruth, anti-truth, and postmodern irrationality. What, then, is our proper response? Should we devote our attention and energies to epistemology and metaphysics? Must we spend ourselves in arguments concerning foundationalism and non-foundationalism? While these issues are not unimportant, they cannot be our central concern. Again, the words of Ryle speak to our age:

> Let no scorn of the world, let no ridicule of smart writers, let no sneers of liberal critics, let no secret desire to please and conciliate the public, tempt us for one moment to leave the old paths, and drop the old practice of enunciating doctrine—clear, distinct, well-defined and sharply-cut doctrine—in all utterances and teachings.[31]

We contend for the objectivity of truth, and we must insist that all persons do actually believe in the objectivity of Truth. The fact is that even the relativists objectivize their own positions. The difference for us is that we know that truth exists in God, who is Truth, and whose Word is truth. Our knowledge is true only in so far as it corresponds with God's revealed truth. We are dependent upon the Word, the Word is not dependent upon us. As Martin Luther stated so clearly, "The objectivity and certainty of the Word remain even if it isn't believed."[32] We have no right to seek refuge in a halfway

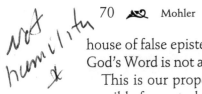
not humility ✗

house of false epistemological humility. To deny the truthfulness of God's Word is not an act of humility, but of unspeakable arrogance.

This is our proper epistemological humility—not that it is not possible for us to know, but that the truth is not our own. We are dependent upon the Word of God. Indeed, we submit ourselves to the Word of God, as believers, teachers, and preachers. And this is genuine knowledge, revealed knowledge. It is knowledge of which we are not ashamed. As Gordon Clark warned:

> If man can know nothing truly, man can truly know nothing. We cannot know that the Bible is the Word of God, that Christ died for our sin, or that Christ is alive today at the right hand of the Father. Unless knowledge is possible, Christianity is non-sensical, for it claims to be knowledge. What is at stake in the twentieth century is not simply a single doctrine, such as the Virgin Birth, or the existence of Hell, as important as those doctrines may be, but the whole of Christianity itself. If knowledge is not possible to man, it is worse than silly to argue points of doctrine—it is insane.[33]

We confess that knowledge is possible, but knowledge of spiritual things is revealed. Without the Word of God we would know nothing of redemption, of Christ, of God's sovereign provision for us. We would have no true knowledge of ourselves, of our sin, of our hopelessness but for the mercy of Christ. As Professor R. B. Kuiper reminded his students, the most direct, the simplest, and most honest answer to the question, "How do you know?" is this: "The Bible tells us so."[34]

As Jesus reminded Peter, immediately after Peter's majestic confession, "Flesh and blood did not reveal this to you, but My Father who is in heaven" (Matt. 16:17). So it is with us: Our true knowledge was not revealed to us by flesh and blood, and certainly was not discovered on our own by the power of our own rationality and insight; it is revealed to us in the Word of God.

This is our proper humility. But we must be on guard against an improper and faithless humility. Wilfred Cantwell Smith has asserted that "it is morally not possible to actually go out into the world and say to devout, intelligent fellow human beings: We believe that we know God and we are right; you believe that you know God, and you are totally wrong."[35] Of course, Smith is correct; we have no right to assert such a statement, in and of ourselves and of our own knowledge. But we have no right *not* to bear witness to the truth of God's Word, and on that basis to proclaim the truths revealed in God's Word.

For this reason, our defense of biblical inerrancy is never a diversion or distraction from our proper task. This is why those who affirm biblical inerrancy and those who deny inerrancy are divided, not by a minor distinction, but by an immense epistemological and theological chasm.

Every aspect of the theological task and every doctrinal issue are affected by the answer to this fundamental question: Is the Bible the authentic, authoritative, inspired, and inerrant Word of God in written form, and thus God's faithful witness to himself? For the believing church, the answer must be yes. With the framers of the Chicago Statement on Biblical Inerrancy, we affirm that "The authority of Scripture is inescapably impaired if this total divine inerrancy is in any way limited or disregarded, or made relative to a view of truth contrary to the Bible's own; and such lapses bring serious loss to both the individual and the Church."[36] We confess and affirm the truthfulness of Scripture in every respect, and we stand under the authority of the Word of God, never over the Word. In other words, we come to the Scriptures, not with a postmodern hermeneutic of suspicion, but with a faithful hermeneutic of submission.

As our Lord stated concerning the Scriptures, "Thy Word is Truth" (John 17:17). And, as Paul wrote to Timothy, "All Scripture is inspired by God and profitable for teaching, for reproof, for correction, for training in righteousness" (2 Tim. 3:16). Made clear in this text is the inescapable truth that our task is to teach and to preach this Word; to reprove, to correct, and to train in righteousness. Should our churches return in faithfulness to this fundamental charge, the secular worldview would lose its grip on the believing church.

Truth's Assault on Modernity

The assault modernity has unleashed on truth has taken its toll—not that modernity has weakened truth, for the truth stands inviolate. Rather, the toll taken by modernity's assault is measured in the increased secularity of the culture and the churches, in the compromised witness of many Christians, in the accommodated messages preached in many pulpits, and in the deadly confusion of the age.

Within the Christian hope is the knowledge that all this will one day be reversed. By God's grace, the imperfect will give way to the perfect, confusion will give way to clarity, modern ideologies will be seen to be empty. Every knee shall bow, and every tongue shall confess, that Jesus Christ is Lord.

And yet even now we can see that, just as modernity has launched its attack on truth, the truths of God's Word are launching an assault upon modernity. To all who have eyes to see, the secular idols of modernity are visibly falling. With the eyes of faith, we see that truth is the hound, and modernity is the hare. Modernity, postmodernity, hypermodernity, and whatever yet may come is evidence of modernity's last gasp. God's truth abideth still.

We confess that all we truly know of God and ourselves, of meaning and life, we know by the revealed Word of God. Thus we acknowledge that without the Word of God, we would be lost and ignorant, blind and hopeless. Our powers of discernment are so limited, and so devastatingly corrupted by sin, that we know nothing of eternal consequence but for the Scriptures, and even here we are dependent upon the illumination of the Holy Spirit for our understanding.

Modern naturalistic scientism claims that "The Cosmos is all that is or ever was or ever will be."[37] But the Word of God declares, "In the beginning God created the heavens and the earth" (Gen. 1:1). Modernity is predicated upon the assumption that the natural order is the product of a cosmic accident: the chance explosion of time, energy, and cosmic dust. The natural order of planets, cells, atoms, and galaxies are objects of scientific study, devoid of any meaning. Yet the Bible asserts that "The heavens are telling the glory of God; and their expanse is declaring the work of His hands" (Ps. 19:1).

In essence, the universe is either meaningful or meaningless. The question hangs on the declaration of a Creator. The Scriptures reveal that nature itself reveals the Creator—even his personal attributes.[38] But this is a knowledge we have corrupted. As Paul wrote to the Romans, we sinners have so corrupted this knowledge that, surveying the creation, we turn to worship the creature rather than the Creator.[39] The naturalistic worldview of modernity insists that human beings are merely a complex order of evolved organisms— simply one animal among other animals, one accident among other accidents. But God's Word reveals that "Then God said, 'Let Us make man in Our image, according to Our likeness; and let them rule over the fish of the sea and over the birds of the sky and over the cattle and over all the earth, and over every creeping thing that creeps upon the earth'"(Gen. 1:26).

Modernity debates whether the world will end with a bang, or with a whimper, exploded by the force of the atom or dissipating into a quiet cosmic entropy. The Word declares that the Lord shall return with a shout, and all things will be brought to consummation by his decree and power.[40] The modern worldview is predicated upon chance and contingency, but the Word of God reveals the unconditional nature of divine providence, that God governs all that occurs and has surrendered none of his power. The modern humanistic worldview assumes and asserts that human beings are basically good, even perfectible. Any undesired behavior is redefined and dismissed as the result of an abusive childhood, environmental deprivation, emotional illness, genetic predisposition, or uncontrollable urges. The awful despotisms of the twentieth century have been driven by utopian visions, attempting to create the "new communist Man" or the *Ubermensch*. At the root of these is the lie of humanism. But the Bible reveals that we are the children of Adam. We bear his mark, in Adam we sinned, and we have sinned on our own, for "all have sinned and fall short of the glory of God" (Rom. 3:23).

In so far as modernity allows for God, it permits the notion of a blithe spirit or a cultural symbol. The rise of new and old paganisms in our mainstream culture is but one indication of the very tangible idolatry in our midst. Americans are not troubled by the presence of non-threatening deities, and will even commercialize their paraphernalia.

Scripture, however, reveals the God of Abraham, Isaac, and Jacob, the Father of our Lord Jesus Christ. This God is jealous and will allow no rivals. He is omnipotent, omniscient, eternal, immutable, personal, transcendent, indivisible, merciful, gracious, and yet filled with wrath against sin. Most supremely, he is holy. He is infinite in all his perfections. It is against this God that we have sinned.

He has revealed himself in his Word as Father, Son, and Holy Spirit—a Trinity of three persons who are yet one. This, too, is a mystery beyond our comprehension, but it is a truth revealed in the Word of Truth.

The modern worldview suggests a message of secular salvation through self-improvement, self-denial, self-gratification, self-empowerment, and self-consciousness. The Bible reveals that salvation is all of grace, and made possible and actual by the shed blood of Jesus Christ, who died as our substitute and the propitiation for our sin.

The Bible reveals to us the truth about God, about ourselves, about our sin and condemnation, about our salvation and redemption, about our sanctification and eventual glorification. We must preach the Word—and the whole truth of the Word.

The sad reality is, however, that modernity's assault upon the truth has taken its toll, not only in the world, but also in the church. Within the organized and culturally recognized church are those whose worldview and doctrinal commitments are more humanistic than the humanists, more naturalistic than the naturalists, and more secular even than some secularists. Vast segments of the organized church in Western societies reflect little more than a thin crust of religious language spread over modernity's most cherished secular assumptions.

Our confidence must be that here, too, the truth is assaulting modernity even as modernity is assaulting the truth. The knowledge that modernity has given birth to a death culture is dawning in enclaves where the light of Scripture may shine but dimly. In some churches and denominations where the maxims of modernity have reigned for most of this century, by God's grace the light may yet again shine. This must be our hope and prayer.

Nevertheless, our primary concern must be to see our own houses are put in order. Evangelical compromise and disarray demand our humility and our urgent prayer for revival, reformation, and renewal. We must take measure of our own doctrinal fidelity and acknowledge the extent to which we have failed to apply the truth of God's Word and to embody that Word in doctrine, worship, and life.

We are not without assistance from the saints who have gone before us. With humility and gratitude we look to the Reformers with the humble acknowledgment that our churches are in need of reformation, even as were the churches of the sixteenth century. Our churches are worldly in lifestyle, worship, and piety. We have too often sacrificed doctrinal clarity on the altar of progress, statistics, and public opinion. We have seen the worship of God too often made into a human-centered entertainment event. We have allowed our confessions of faith to be historic markers rather than living affirmations.

In the spirit of the Reformers, and following their example, let us determine to confess the truths of God's Word—and all the truths of God's Word.

Let us confess *sola Scriptura* and therefore submit ourselves before the truth of the Word of God, preaching, teaching, and applying that Word to all dimensions of life. Let there be no rival authority, and let us never apologize for our confession of the Scriptures—inerrant, inspired, infallible, and unbroken—as our sole authority for knowledge and doctrine.

Let us submit to no other authority, whether a pope, a self-declared prophet, or ubiquitous public opinion. We stand by the Word, even as we stand under the Word.

We also confess *solus Christus,* for we have nothing to claim for our salvation but the mercies and merits of Christ and his atonement. This is all we need, and unspeakably more than we deserve. We must confess Christ—from his preexistence and virgin birth to his exaltation and glorious return. Furthermore, we must confess that Christ is the only Savior, for there is salvation in no other name. Christ's work is sufficient for our redemption and all God intends for us. Nothing can be added to that work or taken from it.

We confess also *sola gratia,* for salvation is by grace alone. Indeed, all that is ours is by grace—even the very knowledge of God. We must resist every effort to rob grace of its simplicity, and thus make of Christ's work a mockery. We are sinners who were spiritually dead, and but for grace would die not only lost but ignorant of our lostness. By grace we have been elected unto salvation by the sovereign act of God. By grace we are kept by the power of God.

We preach justification by faith—the material principle of the Reformation—and thus we confess *sola fide.* By this article the church stands or falls, for justification by faith is the essence of the gospel. To make this assertion is to admit that the contemporary evangelical movement has sadly, tragically, and progressively abdicated justification by faith, and thus in some sectors is preaching a false gospel. We stand by the chief article of the Reformation—not as a historical referent, but as our living confession.

Most important, we confess *sola Deo gloria,* and we pray that in all things God alone will be glorified. To him all glory is due, to him all glory belongs. He is the King of glory. Let us therefore reject the glorification of any substitute, of any rival.

We pray that God will be glorified in our confession, our churches, our discipleship, our preaching, our teaching, our witness, and our living. We must acknowledge that this is a true test of our faithfulness, and perhaps our most essential test.

In an age of untruth, we contend for the truth—knowing that it is not our own, but that truth which is revealed by God in his Word. Such contending calls for a holy boldness wedded to a proper humility. Writing to Emperor Charles V on the necessity of reforming the Church, John Calvin sets a worthy example:

> But be the issue what it may, we will never repent of having begun, and of having proceeded thus far. The Holy Spirit is a faithful and unerring witness to our doctrine. We know, I say, that it is the eternal truth of God that we preach. We are, indeed, desirous, as we ought to be, that our ministry may prove salutary to the world; but to give it this effect belongs to God, not to us.[41]

Indeed, the effect belongs to God, not to us. But we pray for reformation in our midst and in our churches, acknowledging that this will come only by the grace and mercy of our sovereign God. We stand by the truth of God's Word—and the truths of God's Word. The effect belongs to God. *Soli Deo Gloria!*

good chapter

4

Catechesis, Preaching, and Vocation

Gene Edward Veith

hroughout most of the twentieth century, the major theological issue was what has been called "The Battle for the Bible." Beginning with the conflict between the modernists and the fundamentalists, the American church has been torn between those who believe that the teachings of the Bible should be judged according to the latest intellectual and cultural trends and those who believe in the inerrancy of Scripture. Throughout most of the century, liberal theologians, armed with the historical-critical method and the prestige of the intellectual establishment, battled with evangelicals, who insisted on the reality of divine inspiration and a supernatural gospel.

Amid the carnage of denominational schisms, seminary purges, and congregational splits, the modernists seemed to win most of the battles. And yet, as the twentieth century winds to a close, it is evident that, for all practical purposes, the evangelicals won the war.

The mainline Protestant denominations that rejected biblical authority in favor of the various modernist theologies have dwindled in membership and cultural relevance. Evangelicals, on the other hand, who continued to proclaim the life-changing gospel of Christ, have flourished, both in numbers and influence. Although a critical stance toward Scripture continues in academic theology, evangelicals and Catholics dominate the religious life of the nation, while liberal churches are scarcely even players anymore.

But despite this apparent victory, a new theological battle is brewing. It might be called "The Battle for the Gospel." Astonishingly, the attacks on the gospel are coming from the ranks of evangelicals themselves.

Classical Protestantism has always taught that Jesus Christ died to save sinners, but many contemporary evangelicals are downplaying sin, salvation, and the atonement. The new gospel replaces salvation with therapy. Sin gives way to self-esteem; the doctrine of justification by faith is replaced with the doctrine of positive thinking. This new version of Christianity recasts the Bible from the Word of salvation into a step-by-step manual for happy living. The hard edges of historic Christianity—the Bible's stern moral demands, unpleasant doctrines such as hell, Christ as the one way to salvation—are minimized in an effort to reduce Christianity to a feel-good religion. The focus of the new theology is not God, but the self. Objective doctrines are replaced by subjective experiences; worshiping a holy God gives way to entertaining the congregation. Such notions may promote church growth, but they are not historic Christianity.

A curious feature of this new evangelical theology is the way it embraces universalism. Reasoning that a touchy-feely God would not want to condemn anyone eternally—and playing down the notion of original sin—some are teaching that God merely annihilates sinners; others, that there are many paths to God; others, that all are saved, but that those who reject God's love miss out on the abundant life here on earth. One variation of evangelical universalism teaches that only those who consciously reject Christ will be condemned; those who have never had the opportunity to hear the gospel will be saved on account of their ignorance. By this logic, the best way to bring salvation to the world would be to *not* tell anyone about Christ. Thus, evangelicals, whose very name testifies to the centrality of the gospel, deconstruct themselves.

At issue in both the "Battle for the Bible" and the "Battle for the Gospel" is the truth of God's Word. The modernists questioned whether what the Bible said corresponded to the canons of scientific and rationalist truth. Today we face a different dilemma. The modernist trust in science and reason has fallen apart. The postmodernists are questioning not only whether the Bible is objectively true; they are questioning whether there is any objective truth whatsoever.

Christianity, on the contrary, rests on truth. To be sure, our fallen human nature can never comprehend truth fully, and our reason by itself is incapable of knowing God's truth. This is why we need Scripture, God's self-revelation in human language, to understand our lost condition and God's gracious gift of salvation through the cross of Jesus Christ. As Luther says in his Large Catechism, in a passage that refutes the claim that the Reformers and the Protestant confessions did not teach the inerrancy of Scripture, "God does not lie. My neighbor and I—in short, all men—may err and deceive, but God's Word cannot err."[1]

In Gethsemane, Jesus prayed for his followers, asking his Father to "sanctify them through thy truth," significantly adding, "thy word is truth" (John 17:17). For the Christian, truth is not some humanly devised rational system; rather, truth is manifest in the person of Jesus Christ: "I am the way, the truth, and the life." Jesus then immediately testifies to the exclusivity of this truth: "No man cometh unto the Father, but by me" (John 14:6). The Bible also makes clear that Christians must cultivate truth as the basis of their spiritual life and their life in the world. Truth is described as part of the armor of God: "Stand therefore, having your loins girt about with truth" (Eph. 6:14). To gird one's loins meant to get ready for action, to put on one's sword belt. To survive in the world and to engage in spiritual warfare, Christians must be prepared with the truth.

The question is, How can Christians be "girt about with truth" in an age that denies the very possibility of truth? How can the church disciple its members and proclaim the Law and gospel to nonbelievers in a climate of intellectual and moral relativism?

To prepare Christians by girding their loins with truth is actually another way of referring to education. The church has always had its teaching ministry in Bible study and preaching. Historically, the church has also founded schools and universities to educate Christians in the ways of truth.

Although the task of promoting truth in the postmodern age is difficult, certain features of that age offer reasons for hope. As the structures built on the shifting sands of relativism collapse, people will yearn for a foundation built on rock.

Postmodern Times

The modern era, with its Enlightenment rationalists and its scientific materialists, was still interested in truth. Inclined to reject the claims of revelation, modernists sought rational reasons or historical evidence for religious faith. In theology, both modernists and fundamentalists argued over questions of truth: Did the events of the Bible actually take place? Are miracles possible? Was Jesus really the Son of God, and did he physically rise from the dead? Liberal theologians, conditioned by modernism, assumed such supernatural claims were untrue, the product of a "premodern" mind. Conservatives insisted that the miracles of the Bible and the accounts of the history of redemption were true, that God's revelation is a reliable source of knowledge.

Today, modernism, though existing in certain isolated pockets, is all but over. The promises of reason, the notion that the human mind can engineer the perfect society, that science and technological progress can solve all problems, have faded in bitter disillusionment. The reasons for the passing of modernism are complex, ranging from the findings of technical scholarship to the practically universal disenchantment with the bloodshed, tyranny, and corruption of the twentieth century, that "modern age" looked to with such optimism by believers in progress. Around the time of the 1960s, academics were dismantling the claims of reason, and the general public turned away from the apparent meaninglessness of the objective world and began an inward quest for subjective fulfillment.

The postmodernists of both academia and pop culture reasoned that if reason, empiricism, and the pursuit of objective knowledge have proven so disappointing, perhaps the problem is objectivity. Instead of a static, external truth, perhaps truth is only a provisional construction of the individual or the culture. Just as modernism was dominated by the hard sciences, postmodernism is dominated by the social sciences. Beliefs are seen as psychological or sociological phenomena. The way we think is shaped by our culture; there are many different cultures. Who is to say that one culture's interpretation of reality is better than another's? We in the West, with our individualism and scientific worldview, look at Nature in one way; New Guinea tribesmen look at Nature in another way. Who is in better harmony with their environment? On what grounds can we say that our truth—with its heritage of colonialism and ecological destruction—is better than theirs? Social scientists began fostering the notion of cultural relativism, implying that all truth-claims and moral principles are nothing more than cultural constructions and that all are equally valid.

At the same time, existentialism was moving away from the French cafés and artists' garrets into the intellectual and cultural mainstream. For the existentialists, the meaning of life is that there is no meaning. Once a person realizes that there is no ready-made meaning in the universe, it is possible to create a meaning for oneself. An authentic life is one that does not accept the preprogrammed answers of tradition, reason, or religion. By the power of the will, one can choose a meaning for oneself. Whether one chooses Marxism or Christianity, a life of crime or a life of service, meaning is created by an act of the will.

The original existentialists were tormented souls, wrestling with despair. Today's pop existentialists find the lack of objective meaning in life to be liberating. Those who believe in abortion label themselves as "pro-choice." They constitute a definitive example of existential ethics, acknowledging no objective moral principles that apply to all human beings. What makes an action moral is whether there was a choice. If a woman chooses to have a baby, that is right "for her." If a woman chooses to have an abortion, that is right "for her." Any application of transcendent moral absolutes is excluded, as is objective scientific information about the development of the fetus. Whether the issue is the propriety of various "sexual lifestyle choices," "the right to die," or "ethical decision making" as a way of teaching ethics in school, morality is seen as wholly a matter of the will, and all choices are regarded as equally valid.

Today we hear casual epistemological statements that would stagger both classical and modernist philosophers. "That may be true for you," someone says in a discussion of religion, "but it isn't true for me." Every casual discussion seems to end with the mantra, "everyone is entitled to their own beliefs." The assumption is that everyone is locked into their own private virtual realities. Since there are no objective criteria for truth applicable to everyone, attempts to persuade someone to change his or her beliefs are interpreted as oppressive acts of power: "You have no right to impose your beliefs on someone else."

The language of rational assent is replaced by the language of aesthetics. Instead of saying, "I agree with what that church teaches," people say, "I like that church." Instead of saying, "I believe in Jesus," people say, "I like Jesus." Of course, they usually do not "like" the Bible's teachings on sin, hell, and judgment. What they do not like, they do not believe. Truth gives way to pleasure; the intellect is replaced by the will.

When people exclude truth, basing their faith on what they enjoy and what they desire, they can believe in literally anything. This is why affluent, well-educated people are so open to psychic hotlines, crystal vendors, channelers of space aliens, and what would seem like obviously fraudulent New Age gurus. How could anyone believe in such things? The answer, of course, is that truth has nothing to do with postmodernist religious beliefs. Devotees say such things as, "The Maharishi is really cool." Or, "I really like Buddhism." Or, "Scientology really helps me get in touch with my feelings."

Postmodernists tend to be syncretists, putting together elements of different religions or belief systems that they find attractive, ignoring the fact that they may be logically incompatible. The postmodernist mind tends to be so compartmentalized that it can hold two mutually contradictory ideas at the same time.

A pastor told me about a young man in his congregation who was very devout, believing strongly in Christ and the Bible. But he also believed in reincarnation. He thought it would really be cool to come back in another life.

After arguing with him but getting nowhere, the pastor finally decided to set him straight. "You do believe in the Bible, right?" he asked.

"Sure," the young man replied.

The pastor sat down with him, took out a Bible, and had him look up Hebrews 9:27: "It is appointed unto men once to die, but after this the judgment."

"So, you can see," said the pastor, "that the Bible clearly teaches that we aren't reincarnated. We die one time, and then we are judged. The dead don't come back, but are sent to either heaven or hell. That's what it says, right? 'It is appointed unto men once to die, but after this the judgment.'"

The young man paused a minute. Then he said, "Well, that's your interpretation."

Though the young man had never heard of postmodernist hermeneutics, he was a master practitioner. There are no facts, only interpretations. The plainest evidence can be explained away, and a person is free to accept any interpretation that is most pleasing.

Postmodernist Education

How can the church proclaim its message when truth itself is dismissed as irrelevant? How can relativists be made to pay attention to the truths of God's Word?

Clearly, this young man's capacity to believe in two contradictory worldviews simultaneously and his inability to acknowledge objective truth is, very literally, a crisis of belief. The problem is not just that he is believing the wrong things; the problem is that he does not know what belief is. Although Christian belief is never merely the function of a logical argument, depending as it does on the revelation of the Holy Spirit, believing does involve some intellectual processes and an objective content. But people who grow up in the postmodern age are ill-equipped to deal with objective ideas.

dealing with objective idea

[handwritten margin annotations: Process, Knowledge, feeling, fact, socialization, Truth]

Chances are, this young man went to a school that, under the influence of Dewey and other progressive educators, stressed processes over knowledge, feelings over facts, socialization over truth. He learned the process of reading from textbooks designed to be entertaining rather than challenging. He probably spent a lot of class time in groups, sharing his feelings about American history and clarifying his values about social problems.

If he went to college, he would learn about cultural relativism, group oppression, and the virtues of pluralism. In grad school he would learn how to deconstruct texts and how objective meaning is, at best, an illusion, and at worst, an imposition of power. Even if he did not go to college, the culture-creators did—those who make the television shows, run the entertainment industry, write the newspapers, teach in the schools, and otherwise manufacture the intellectual climate we imbibe with the air we breathe.

Education has always sought to equip young people to deal with truth. Today, with some exceptions, this is no longer the case. Instead, postmodernist education works to undermine the capacity for truth.

The young man who believes in both the Bible and reincarnation would not necessarily get much help in thinking clearly from the church. The anti-intellectual strain in American Christianity has, for most of the century, favored the heart over the head, giving experience priority over doctrine and encouraging individualistic pietism over the corporate life of the church. Today, the American church is reaping the bitter fruit of this anti-intellectualism, as its members are left helpless against the onslaught of anti-Christian relativism.

[handwritten margin annotation: Here here]

To recover and build on the truths of God's Word, the church must rehabilitate the Christian mind. Not only theologians and pastors but laypeople as well must be equipped to think in terms of truth. In finding a way to do this, the contemporary church can take some lessons from its own history.

Premodern Relativism

While relativism may be postmodern, it is not particularly new. The notion that truth is unknowable, that morality varies from cul-

Liberal Arts Education

for free citizens

ture to culture, and that there are no absolutes was first articulated in ancient Greece by the Sophists. In reaction, Socrates rose up to show that there are indeed absolutes, thereby, with Plato and Aristotle, founding classical philosophy.

When classical civilization was exhausted, relativism returned with the Stoics, Epicureans, and the cultural diversity of the Roman Empire. This may well be reflected in Pilate's comment, "What is truth?" (John 18:38), when the Truth was standing right in front of him. This era, which entertained itself with sex and violence and tolerated all religions except Christianity, turned out to be the greatest age of the church, which not only remained faithful but converted the whole empire to Christ.

The early church was not market-driven. It did not make Christianity particularly user-friendly. Non-Christians could attend the preaching service, but they had to leave when Holy Communion was celebrated. Converts had to go through extensive, lengthy catechesis and examination before they were accepted for baptism. In the ultimate barrier to new member assimilation, those who did become Christians faced the death penalty. Nevertheless, by the power of the Holy Spirit, the church grew like wildfire.

When Rome fell to the Barbarians and the empire collapsed into anarchy, the church was one of the few institutions to survive. As the Vandals were burning the libraries, the church was busy preserving even the secular knowledge of classical civilization, copying manuscripts, cultivating scholarship, and operating schools. Eventually, the invading pagan hordes were themselves converted to Christianity, and the foundation was laid for the High Middle Ages.

To combat the ungodly philosophies of the late Roman Empire and the primitive paganism of the Barbarians, the early church developed what would be known as a liberal arts education. The term "liberal" derives from the Latin word for freedom. For the Greeks and Romans, a "liberal" education was that suited for free citizens; mere occupational training was for slaves. Those who were free, on the other hand, needed to know how to think. The early church took the best of classical learning and combined it with a Christian worldview.

Contrary to the common assumption, the liberal arts education that brought Europe through the Dark Ages was not merely a continuation of the Greek and Roman schools. The Seven Liberal Arts, as a systematic educational program, was in large measure a Christian invention. While drawing on the ancient learning, the liberal arts were systematized by the church in light of Augustine's critique of classical thought. It was the Christian scholar and statesman Cassiodorus who first put forward the notion of the Seven Liberal Arts before his death in A.D. 575.[2]

The combination of evangelism, education, and cultural reformation transformed the ancient world, which was not unlike our own. Pagan practices such as abortion and infanticide were stopped. The brutal amusement of blood sports came to an end. Rampant sexual immorality, violent feuds, and moral anarchy submitted to God's Law.

Eventually, medieval civilization also stagnated. Although not relativistic as such, the church of the Late Middle Ages—again, not unlike today—was succumbing to superstition, worldliness, and human-centeredness. Education had become reduced to the mastery of highly technical, specialized trivia, a system of certification for elite professionals, with most of the population lapsing into illiteracy. Not unlike today.

The Renaissance was essentially a revival of classical education. The Reformation began at a liberal arts university at Wittenberg and was spread by classical scholars such as Melanchthon, Zwingli, and Calvin. Once the Reformation was underway, education became a major religious priority. Schools were opened to teach the laity how to read God's Word. Ministers conducted catechism classes and preached sermons to explain the truths of sin and grace, and the new teachings began to be reflected throughout the culture in art, music, literature, and social life. Once more, the church took up the task of teaching its members how to think biblically.

The Reformation of Education

Bringing back truth—specifically, the truth of God's Word—is an educational task. As it did in the days of the early church and the

Protestant Reformation, the church must again take up its teaching ministry, training Christians to think biblically and to influence the culture as a whole with God's truth.

One of today's most promising movements in educational reform is, for the most part, led by Christians. It is a recovery of classical, liberal arts education, teaching the same disciplines of mind used by the early church and the Reformation to cultivate God's truth.

With the manifest failures of public education, many Christians are starting schools of their own or teaching their children at home. Such efforts are in the best tradition of the Christian intellectual heritage. Often, though, these schools or homeschools simply add on religious instruction to what is essentially a secular, postmodernist curriculum.

Even when the curriculum is heavily loaded with conservative ideology, Christian teaching, and moral indoctrination, the teaching methods and educational philosophy often follow the same methodology advocated by contemporary educational theorists. School is designed to be fun. The emphasis is experiential rather than intellectual, with "learning experiences" given priority over logical analysis. There is usually lots of coloring, group work, and "sharing times." A popular notion among homeschoolers is "learning as play."

I do not mean to denigrate these efforts by Christian teachers and parents to give children a better education than they would receive in the public schools. In most cases, they are immeasurably superior to what is offered by the contemporary educational establishment, and the addition of Christian training and the biblical worldview can be extraordinarily salutary. But experiential, subjective, affective learning is essentially postmodernist. A subjectivist methodology can undermine the best-intentioned efforts to teach objective content. What is needed is a different educational philosophy—and one is at hand: the classical liberal arts.

Douglas Wilson and his Association of Classical and Christian Schools have brought back the kind of education that gave us Augustine, Luther, Newton, and most of the other great minds of Western civilization.[3] Despite what many college catalogues say, a liberal arts education means more than just a broad education with lots of requirements in different fields. The liberal arts is a specific program that offers a coherent, sequential approach to learning and thinking, and it is now being employed in scores of Christian schools and by hundreds of homeschoolers.

Classical education is built upon the *trivium* of grammar, logic, and rhetoric. To learn a language, one must master the basic structures and vocabulary that constitute its grammar. Then, one must learn to think in that language, corresponding to the stage of logic. Then, one must learn to express oneself effectively in the language, the stage of rhetoric. But the *trivium* is not just a matter of language; it applies to all subjects and corresponds to the three basic realms of human thought.

"Grammar" refers to foundational factual knowledge; "logic," also known as "dialectic," refers to the ability to think, process ideas, analyze concepts, raise questions, and draw conclusions; "rhetoric" refers to original expression, the ability to put forward one's own ideas in a persuasive way. The *trivium* thus can be thought of as knowledge, thought, and expression, or the combination of facts, reasoning, and creativity.

There is a grammar, logic, and rhetoric in every subject. The grammar of math would be memorizing the multiplication table and mastering the basic concepts and skills. The logic of math would be the ability to think mathematically and to solve problems. The rhetoric of math would be the ability to invent mathematical solutions for one's own needs. The grammar of science would be the foundational truths of the natural order; its logic would be the scientific method; its rhetoric would be original research. The grammar of history would be the names, dates, and events; its logic would be the ability to think about history, to draw patterns and determine causes and effects; its rhetoric might involve applying the lessons of history or conducting fresh investigations into the past.

Even today most of the professions retain traces of their origins in the liberal arts: Physicians learn the basics of anatomy and physiology in the first years of medical school; then they go on rounds with a doctor who, in the classical dialectical manner, asks them questions, training them how to think about disease. Finally, as interns, they proceed to the rhetoric stage: making their own diagnoses and prescribing their own courses of treatment. Attorneys, too, first cram knowledge; then their professors use the time-honored Socratic method of the liberal arts dialectic, asking them questions and making them think; finally, they can argue cases on their own.

This pattern of acquiring information, learning how to think about it, and then expressing one's knowledge in original ways is the conceptual framework for all genuine learning. According to Douglas Wilson and the new classicists, it is also a developmental model. In the early grades—even today called "grammar school" from the days of classical education—children learn best by memorization, and so they acquire a vast appetite for facts, objective information, and the other facets of grammar. In the middle school years, young people start to ask questions, wondering "why?" and "how?" and even challenging authority. This is the time to teach them logic. In the high school years, teenagers start to be expressive; preoccupied with their new sense of identity and the growth of their emotions, they want to be understood. This is the time to teach them rhetoric.

The *trivium* gives a foundation for learning, a mental discipline for apprehending and employing truth. Once the *trivium* is mastered, a student can go on to the advanced and more specialized subjects that constitute the *quadrivium:* music, arithmetic, astronomy, and geometry. These subjects, corresponding roughly to university education, can be construed more broadly as kinds of truth: Music would include aesthetic truths, the perception of the ordered harmony of beauty, which was seen not as mere subjective pleasure but as an absolute. Arithmetic would include the mathematical absolutes built into the universe and into pure thought. Astronomy would involve all of the empirical sciences, the truths perceived by the senses and by external evidence. Geometry would include architecture and design, the spatial relations that are implicit in both engineering and the visual arts.

Today's classical schools use the *trivium* and the *quadrivium* as conceptual models to structure their entire curriculum, even as they study more conventional subjects. Classical schools typically teach the three R's, civics, history, biology, and the like, but they do it in a different way than the public schools, using the *trivium* to study them in a more thorough, systematic way. Classical schools also typically teach Latin and feature heavy doses of great literature. The Association of Classical and Christian Schools also teaches religion, with Bible and theology studied with similar systematic rigor and integrated into the whole curriculum.

Whenever Western civilization reaches a state of stagnation, someone rediscovers classical education and the result is cultural rejuvenation. The golden age of Athens, the Roman Republic, the High Middle Ages, the Renaissance and Reformation, and the Enlightenment were all sparked by classicism and the rediscovery of the liberal arts. Surely the time is right in our present cultural moment for another Renaissance.

Not all of these movements, of course, were Christian, though today it is mostly Christians who are promoting classical education. No doubt this is because Christians are among the few today who have a conceptual basis for truth. Educational reform is not the same as spiritual revival. Nevertheless, the recovery of the habits of mind that recognize truth is an educational task of monumental proportions, one in which the church has a vital interest. As it has in the past, the church—through its network of schools and colleges and its community influence—may once again find itself the major patron of quality education in an essentially illiterate culture.

But how can the church promote the truths of God's Word in its own teaching ministry? This will require a new emphasis on catechesis and, as in the Reformation, a resurgence of biblical preaching.

Catechesis

The way the church has historically trained its members to know and to understand Christian doctrine is the process of catechesis. Children and new members would typically learn the Ten Commandments, the Lord's Prayer, and the Apostles' Creed. Then, the minister would ask them questions about what these foundational texts mean. So prepared, they would confess their faith publicly. This kind of instruction was based on the *trivium*. Memorizing creeds

If you show "rotten" you are "rotten"

and Bible verses is grammar; the dialectic of questions and answers is the methodology of logic; this process was designed to equip young Christians for their confirmation, when they would make their own profession of faith (the stage of rhetoric).

The great catechisms of the major confessional traditions—such as Luther's Small and Large Catechisms and the Westminster Catechism—are models of lucid, profound thinking about the implications of Christian truth. In churches that still bother to use catechisms, they are often relegated to the grammar stage, the questions and answers memorized, if not fully understood. While memorizing the catechism is a worthy project—we need more grammar than ever these days—the question-and-answer format attests to the need recognized by the confessors who wrote the catechisms that Christians need to learn how to think about their faith.

Churches today do not always have catechism classes as such, but catechetical instruction does take place in Sunday schools, Bible classes, and informal Bible studies. Christian education has become a major emphasis in many parishes, which often have a full-time director of Christian education and elaborate programs for children and adults. With this infrastructure, churches should aim at teaching the truths of God's Word by helping their parishioners know the facts of Scripture, think Christianly, and internalize what they have learned so they can apply it to their everyday lives. They need the grammar, logic, and rhetoric of Christian truth.

Often today Christian education consists mostly of more games and sharing times for both children and adults. Our postmodernist times have been called "the therapeutic" generation, and many classes are modeled on therapy sessions, whether addressed to people with specific problems or aimed at self-disclosure for its own sake. While personal involvement and fellowship with other Christians is valuable and while intimate prayer groups, social activities, and ministries to people with problems should be encouraged, they are no substitute for catechesis in "the Word of truth."

Effective catechesis in an age of relativism must involve remedial education. Just as membership classes usually include instruction in how Christianity is different from other religions and how that particular church body is different theologically from other denominations, Christian education will need to teach how God's Word is in conflict with the trends of the culture. Christian educators must thus teach the distinctiveness of both the biblical worldview and the current cultural worldview, and how to tell the difference between them.

Preaching the Truth of God's Word

More central even than Christian education is the pastor's call to preach God's Word. The pulpit sets the tone for what takes place on every level of the local church, and the battle to recover truth must ultimately be waged by means of the pastor's sermons, in which God promises that the Holy Spirit himself will be at work.

The temptation to preach what people want to hear is always great, but today it has become in some circles almost a homiletical principle. My own pastor tells of attending a church growth conference in which he was told, "Don't preach sin anymore. People don't want to hear that. You need to give them a positive message." Of course, people have never wanted to hear about sin. Repentance hurts. And yet people need to hear God's demands, particularly now in this age of moral relativism; we need to be convicted of sin, so that we can turn in faith to God's forgiveness in Jesus Christ.

What people do want to hear, according to the church growth consultants, is practical tips for successful living. I once heard a sermon entitled "Fifteen Steps to Having a Happy Christmas." It consisted of various principles, extracted out of context from the Bible, for getting along with relatives, managing one's time, and dealing with stress. Not once did it mention the Christ Child and why he came.

Instead of following the cultural trends, a better approach in preaching is to counter them. Media critic Neil Postman has argued for what he calls a "thermostatic" approach to culture.[4] When it gets too cold, a thermostat will kick on the heat; when it gets too hot, a thermostat will turn on the air conditioner. The thermostat does the opposite of the prevailing climate and thus creates a liveable temperature. Postman applies this analogy to education: When a society is hide-bound and static, education can loosen things up by challenging or stretching the status quo; when society is in a state of constant change and instability—as it is today—education needs to conserve traditional ideas.

What is true of education is also true of the church. Those who do not want to be told they are sinners have a special need to hear God's Law. Those who want to hear about how they can be happy need to hear about bearing the cross. To be most relevant, a sermon should preach against the culture.

The tendency today is to pick and choose teachings from the Bible that correspond to our likes and interests. But the test of following the Bible is accepting what goes against one's personal preferences. The Bible is thermostatic, humbling the exalted and exalting the humble (Luke 14:11), and so should our sermons be.

Ultimately, though, a sermon will contain only two messages: the Law and the gospel. Each must convey the truths of God's Word.

The truth of the Law must be preached in all its severity. The preaching of the Law is not mere moralism, however. The temptation is to water down God's transcendent, all-consuming demands so that they are more easily fulfilled. This only creates self-righteousness, which is the greatest barrier to faith in the gospel. Moralistic preaching can easily become self-congratulatory, giving the congregation smug reassurance about how good they are. Such preaching creates not Christians but hypocrites.

The purpose of proclaiming the Law in a sermon should be the conviction of sin. Our postmodernist age manages to be somehow both extremely immoral and extremely self-righteous at the same time. Everyone vehemently denies that they are doing anything wrong.

Instead of a realistic view of sin, which acknowledges the web of evil we are all caught up in by virtue of our fallen nature, advocates of postmodernist ethics want everyone to feel good about themselves. Sin is merely a lifestyle choice, and nothing and no one is really bad. Ultimately, moral relativism is just another manifestation of our human penchant for self-righteousness. Intellectual relativism, too, is nothing more than a self-righteous exaltation of personal preference over created facts. Postmodernists make them-

Truth

selves the lawgiver and the creator, so that there is no need for redemption.

The truth of God's Law stands, despite all the evasions and pathetic attempts at self-justification. The vehemence of the post-modernists in insisting upon their virtue is evidence that the Law does strike a nerve, that guilt is not so easily dismissed and rela-tivized. The preaching of God's objective, transcendent Law and its condemnation of the specific sins of relativism and self-righteous-ness is only a prelude to proclaiming the real solution to the post-modernist condition, the truth of the gospel.

def

In the last analysis, truth is not a human system, or a rationalist ideology, and certainly not a private opinion; rather, truth is the person of Jesus Christ. On the cross, Truth was crucified, objec-tively, outside ourselves. With him, our relativism, subjective expe-riences, and attempts to evade truth are put to death, nailed to that objective tree.

In the same way, our sins—both our sinful actions and our sin-ful condition—are *objectively* removed from us. Ours is an *objective* atonement, which means that we do not have to rely on our change-able moods and experiences, our illusions and petty choices. Because Jesus is the Truth, we are liberated from our unstable, reinvented selves. When Jesus *objectively* rose from the dead, our salvation was won, not as a subjective interpretation, but as a fact.

Preach the truth of the Law and the truth of this gospel, against all pressure, and the barriers against Christianity, no matter how for-midable they seem, will, like the walls of Jericho, come tumbling down.

Vocation

Instead of naively following the trends or constantly playing catch-up to the unbelievers, Christians might well start setting some trends of their own. Historically, Christianity has always influenced culture. From the abolition of infanticide and death-sports in the Roman Empire to the mitigation of political tyranny and the pro-motion of universal education in more recent centuries, the church—

without confusing its sphere with that of the state—has been a leavening influence in every culture in which its presence has been known. When, on the other hand, culture influences Christianity, the result has always been the various brands of liberalism. When the church passively allows the world to set its agenda, the result has always been worldliness, pagan state-worship, spiritual impotence, and sheer irrelevance.

The practical reclamation of truth is not only a theological but also a cultural task. The church must stop being shaped by the culture and once again start shaping the culture. This does not mean that the church should try to take over the kingdoms of this world— that would mean more of the kind of cultural religion we have today. For Christians to influence the world with the truth of God's Word requires the recovery of the great Reformation doctrine of vocation. Christians are called to God's service not only in church professions but also in every secular calling. The task of restoring truth to the culture depends largely on our laypeople.

To bring back truth, on a practical level, the church must encourage Christians to be not merely consumers of culture but *makers* of culture. The church needs to cultivate Christian artists, musicians, novelists, filmmakers, journalists, attorneys, teachers, scientists, business executives, and the like, teaching its laypeople the sense in which every secular vocation—including, above all, the callings of husband, wife, and parent—is a sphere of Christian ministry, a way of serving God and neighbor that is grounded in God's truth. Christian laypeople must be encouraged to be leaders in their fields, rather than eager-to-please followers, working from the assumptions of their biblical worldview, not the vapid clichés of pop culture.

Today's postmodern culture may seem formidable, but it is floundering and sterile, admittedly without basis and without direction. Christian culture-makers, whether as artists or as parents, do have a basis and a direction. Through their creativity, high standards, and sense of vocation, Christian laity, properly prepared and supported, may well bring back truth into the culture.

Another Way to Be Postmodern

Confessing Christians can take heart that relativism is not the only trend of contemporary thought. There are, in fact, two ways of being postmodern. One response to the demise of modernity, with its scientific rationalism, is to reject objective truth altogether. But another response is to go back before modernity, rediscovering the past and bringing what was of value from the premodern era into the present.

While many postmodernist artists are jettisoning objective beauty in favor of shock and pornography, other artists are not only rejecting the rationalist abstractionism of modern art; they are returning to classicism, realism, and the great artistic traditions of Western culture. Instead of bulldozing old buildings, as in modernist urban renewal, cities are restoring them to their original splendor. Brandnew homes are being built that follow the designs of the Victorian era. While some theologians are rejecting truth, others are responding to the end of modernity by going back to the Church Fathers.[5]

Whether in retro-fashions, nostalgia television, or classical realist paintings, there is a new openness to the past. In the disenchantment with the modern, the new is no longer considered better than the old, and time-tested ideas—such as Christianity—assume a new relevance. And in the manifest failures of postmodernism—the chaos, nihilism, and despair that it breeds—many are looking for an alternative. With classicism in education and confessionalism in Christianity, those who believe in truth are now on the cutting edge.

We are calling the church,

amidst our dying culture,

to repent of its worldliness,

to recover and confess the truth of

God's Word

as did the Reformers,

and to see that truth embodied

in doctrine, worship, and life.

5

The *Sola*'s of the Reformation

Michael S. Horton

ll attempts to interpret the past," wrote H. Richard Niebuhr, "are indirect attempts to understand the present and its future."[1] While there has always been a fairly deep antipathy in American culture toward the past and an obsession with the present and the future, Christianity is a religion dedicated to remembering. Again and again in Scripture, especially in the Psalms, believers are called upon to remember what they believe, why they believe it, and to pass the stories of redemptive history down to their children. The prophets do not simply encourage blind optimism toward the future, an attitude that permeates modern society, but rather recall the people of God to their theological roots: "This is what the LORD says: 'Stand at the crossroads and look; ask for the ancient paths, ask where the good way is, and walk in it, and you will find rest for your souls'" (Jer. 6:16). All too often, even believers search for that spiritual rest in a frenzied

99

delight in the new and improved rather than in the tried and tested. As goes the culture, so goes the church these days and in this time and place, in the words of Walter Lippmann earlier this century, "Whirl is king."[2]

Many mainline Protestant denominations that evangelicals left were rich with a heritage that had commanded the intellects, emotions, and actions of generations. Rooted in a sense of institutional and confessional identity, these denominations had lost their confidence in the ability of that heritage to explain and help them cope with the massive changes in modern life. And if there was little left of the classic creedal and confessional integrity of these bodies, there was nothing left for their sons and daughters to pass on to their children. They either became unchurched or joined the evangelical movement, but in either case one wonders if they escaped secularization.

Mainline Protestantism lost its members because it turned its back on its rich resources; evangelical Christianity has tended to gain its members precisely because it never, at least self-consciously, possessed them. It was not simply the case that the liberals followed the culture while the conservatives followed the Bible, but that both were more deeply shaped by the culture than by their confessions.

According to the infamous slogan of the National Council of Churches, "The church follows the world's agenda," but evangelicals show, by their slavish devotion to popular culture, that they, too, have "exchanged the glory of the immortal God for images" (Rom. 1:22). George Barna, for instance, coaches us, "It is critical that we keep in mind a fundamental principle of Christian communication: the audience, not the message, is sovereign."[3] Such sentiments could just as easily have rolled off the lips of Harry Emerson Fosdick seventy years ago. As a *Newsweek* article describes the churches in our day, specifically including evangelicals, "They have developed a 'pick and choose' Christianity in which individuals take what they want . . . and pass over what does not fit their spiritual goals. What many have left behind is a pervasive sense of sin."[4]

It is precisely because modern American evangelicalism does not possess this creedal, confessional heritage that it is capable of exploiting the individualism, romanticism, moralism, and pragmatism of our market-driven culture. While liberal Protestants could only become nominal culture-Christians by explicitly rejecting their confessional commitments, what is to keep evangelicals from easily accommodating when there is but a minimalist view of doctrinal obligations in the first place? Happily, many of these men and women who left mainline churches recovered a sense of appreciation for God's Word in the newly formed evangelical coalition, but they shared with their non-evangelical counterparts a suspicion of the institutional church, tradition, authority, creed, confession, catechism, doctrine, and liturgy—in other words, the disciplines of churchly life. This essentially modern spirit is largely responsible for the unwillingness on the part of many evangelicals, like liberals, to locate "Beth' Els," signposts or markers of God's faithfulness in the past to help direct the church in the present and future. Evangelicals, in fact, are regularly having their chain jerked of late by mainline liberals. In *Leadership Journal*, Duke University theologian William Willimon observed with some sarcasm,

> I'm a mainline-liberal-Protestant-Methodist-type Christian. I know we're soft on Scripture. Norman Vincent Peale has exercised a more powerful effect on our preaching than St. Paul. Listen to us on Sunday, and Leo Buscaglia or Mr. Rogers' Neighborhood may come to mind before you think of Matthew, Mark, Luke or John. I know we play fast and loose with Scripture. But I've always had this fantasy that somewhere, like in Texas, there were preachers who preached it all, Genesis to Revelation, without blinking an eye. . . . Do you know how disillusioning it has been for me to realize that many of these self-proclaimed biblical preachers now sound more like liberal mainliners than liberal mainliners?[5]

Willimon points out two areas in particular where this influence of modernity is detected: "Psychology is God" and "Politics is God." In his book, *Preaching to the Baptized,* Willimon challenges both liberals and evangelicals to recover the content of Christianity and to stop accommodating everything to the lowest common denominator. Similarly, Yale's George Lindbeck writes,

> The leaders of the Enlightenment . . . were not believers, but they were biblically literate and biblically cultured. Conversely, Bible-believing fundamentalists sometimes know remarkably little of the

No Cross

content of scripture. . . . When I first arrived at Yale, even those who came from nonreligious backgrounds knew the Bible better than most of those now who come from churchgoing families. . . . Playing fast and loose with the Bible needed a liberal audience in the days of Norman Vincent Peale, but now, as the case of Robert Schuller indicates, professed conservatives eat it up.[6]

H. Richard Niebuhr laid open the barrenness of liberalism in his clever description of its essential message: "A God without wrath brought men without sin into a kingdom without judgment through the ministrations of a Christ without a Cross."[7] If we think about it, that characterizes much of the evangelical diet these days, although it was intended to describe liberalism in the first half of this century. Often in our time, those who are pointing out the strange capitulation of the churches, including evangelical churches, to the marketplace of secularism are the secular philosophers, sociologists, and popular commentators or mainline liberals who have reached the dead end. With few exceptions, the most trenchant critiques roll off secular or mainline Protestant rather than evangelical presses. It is more frequently those outside the evangelical community who ask the probing question, "Where is that theology of the Reformation, that put meat on the bones of men and women?" Columbia University historian Eugene Rice says that the Reformation "measures the gulf between the secular imagination of the twentieth century and the sixteenth century's intoxication with the majesty of God."[8] We need to repent of our worldliness, and recover and confess our faith as did the Reformers.

Why the Reformers? Surely the early Christians faced the temptation to pare off the rough edges and blunt the offense of the cross. After all, their very lives were at stake, and the "superapostles," as Paul identifies those who wished to make Christianity more attractive by removing the offense of the cross, were constantly undermining the biblical gospel. In the process of appealing to the "felt needs" of Greek "seekers," Paul says, practical wisdom and signs and wonders had replaced the preaching of sin and grace (1 Cor. 1:18–2:5).

But the Protestant Reformation is another important marker. The Reformers, too, faced their own mystics in the form of the Enthusiasts who, in Luther's reference to Muntzer, thought they had "swallowed the Spirit feathers and all." While insisting they followed the Bible, in actual practice they were more apt to follow their own imaginations and private experiences. Calvin, in fact, argued that the Radical Anabaptists and Rome shared more in common than either group shared with genuine apostolic Christianity.[9] The Reformation was certainly the most eventful debate over the nature of salvation and the basic message of Scripture than at any time since the first five centuries, and from it we inherit the label "evangelical."

If we are convinced that the Protestant Reformation was the greatest recovery of the gospel since the time of the apostles and that it left us with a treasury whose riches await rediscovery by a new generation, then surely a new reformation represents a goal for us. It is not that we want to simply replay the Reformation, but that we want to recover and confess the faith as the Reformers did in their time. It is the same message, but it is we now who must step up to the plate. We are not only *confessional* (that is, bound to believe, preach, and teach that which our confessions set forth), but *confessing*. It is not merely a commitment to a past fidelity, although it is that, but it is also *our* confession in *this* time and place. Our world, surrounded by new fears and false hopes, requires a new confession—not new in its message, but fresh in its delivery.

To that end, we affirm the "*sola*'s" (only's) of the Reformation: "only Scripture," "only Christ," "only grace," "only faith," and "to God alone be glory." We are similarly convinced that each of these declarations is threatened even within the very movement that stands in a line of direct spiritual descent from the Reformation. Therefore, we, like our forebears, must make our confession before the church and the world. In what follows, I focus our attention on these key points of the Reformation and draw some conclusions about where we are on each of these "*sola*'s" in our own setting.

Sola Scriptura

While the medieval church embraced a high doctrine of Scripture, in actual practice human wisdom and speculation often set a

It works!

Reinforces The "autonomous self"

priori conditions on what could and could not be drawn from the biblical text, even when the clear intention of various passages contradicted that position.

Whereas speculative metaphysics obscured Scripture in the medieval church, today it is often the speculative behavioral and social sciences that claim priority in contemporary discussion. Thus, even where a high doctrine of inspiration is maintained, the biblical categories of sin and grace are often replaced with therapeutic categories, such as dysfunction and recovery, or the "is" of statistical averages defining the "ought" of ecclesial health. In an effort to be relevant, "contextualization" often becomes an excuse for compromise, realized or not, and this is due not only to a lack of serious theological reflection, but also to the numbing effects of modernity. Few actually declare that they are going to march to a different drummer, but the theological shallowness of evangelicalism is hardly a match for the incessant stream of consciousness that gushes from the broken cisterns of modern and postmodern society.

Beyond pop psychology, marketing and sociological factors are often allowed to define the mission, message, and ministry of the church and individual believers. The spiritual entrepreneur is the hero; the biblical prophet, the villain. Those who interrupt the band with questions are relegated to the fringes, while the most exotic brands of enthusiasm are accorded a place in the mainstream of the movement. And why? Americans need only one reason: It works. Doubtless, other Christian gatherings just now are filling stadiums across the country, imitating popular culture and downplaying the serious themes we are calling the church to recover. Our gathering will not be considered significant by comparison, if significance is measured in secular, pragmatic terms.

All of this combines to create a religion every bit as anthropocentric as that against which the Reformation reacted, although the nature of this challenge is distinctly modern. For Enlightenment intellectuals, the self is autonomous via reason and experience. John Wesley accommodated this Enlightenment vision by arguing that the criteria for determining truth were tradition, reason, and experience, in addition to Scripture. The Romanticism that followed the Enlightenment made man the measure by virtue of his feelings. And for many evangelicals, these powerful forces—especially the Romantic spirit that dominates our age more now than ever—reduce God to the status of a modern monarch, in appearance mighty, in reality powerless. He may bless, but never judge. This is why there seems to be no crisis of confrontation, a sense of urgency and expectancy in God's address. And this is perhaps one reason why so many seek for other "words" and other "wonders" that promise to restore this sense of God's presence. How, then, do we recover the sufficiency of Scripture for doctrine and godliness?

First, we must distinguish things heavenly from things earthly. Here the Reformers were quite helpful in stressing that although in things heavenly the unregenerate person is blind and incapable of finding the truth of the gospel, in things earthly he or she is capable of wisdom, creativity, justice, and even civil righteousness. Therefore, we can expect much truth from secular writers, artists, musicians, philosophers, and scientists in their descriptions of things below. Indeed, the Reformation was in many respects a product of the Renaissance. Furthermore, we are free as Christians in these areas to write secular books, to make secular movies, to compose secular music, to find a secular vocation, and to freely associate with non-Christians in secular environments.

Politics, the arts, literature, science, and even sports and entertainment are all legitimate, if kept in their proper bounds. An owner of a business is free to be pragmatic in determining how to improve profit margins and to employ marketing strategies. Further, a Christian who happens to be an elected official need not fear making political compromises from time to time in order to seek policies that he or she thinks will, in the long run, better serve the public. Such approaches are appropriate to these activities. The problem comes when we confuse these legitimate gifts of creation with the saving arena of redemption. Compromise and pragmatic considerations may not necessarily be sinful in the secular arena, but they are utterly corrosive when questions of ultimate truth are at stake. It is not when Christians exercise their citizenship, read an Updike novel, explore the solar system, and take in a football game, movie, or concert that they are necessarily unfaithful, but it is when their discipleship, evangelism, and worship reflect the obsessions of this passing age rather than "the city without foundations, whose builder and maker is God."

The medieval church, the Reformers argued, had confused things heavenly with things earthly. So, ironically, when there was a question about salvation, Aquinas reached for Aristotle, and yet the realm of common grace and culture was dominated by the church. This same ironic inversion exists in the church today, where we are often shaped by psychology, marketing, sociology, and entertainment in our faith and discipleship at the same time that we substitute participation in secular learning and culture for the building of our evangelical subculture. In short, we are, like the medieval church, of the world but not in it.

The second thing we must do to recover the sufficiency of Scripture is to challenge the rampant individualism and enthusiastic claims of popular spiritual movements.

As the Reformers faced the Roman challenges to the Bible's clarity and sufficiency, the Anabaptists undermined *sola Scriptura* as well by appeals to extrabiblical revelation and by creating a host of individualistic sects led by charismatic prophets. In our day, too, the Word and Spirit are often set against each other in what is often sadly called "revival." Erroneous views of guidance and claims to direct revelation from the Spirit assist in this, but mainstream evangelicals are often as likely as charismatics to rely on subjective experiences, personal feelings, and preferences, reflecting their debt to a commercial culture. In fact, mainline Protestants are more likely than even the unchurched to affirm the statement that "there is no such thing as absolute truth," but evangelicals are not far behind, as they are almost equally divided between those who strongly agree and strongly disagree with the statement.[10] While affirming a high view of Scripture on paper, are we subverting the practical normativity of God's voice in Scripture?

Too often the Protestant view is confused with such individualism. Luther, however, declared, "This would mean that each man would go to hell in his own way," and no one can read Luther, Calvin, or any of the other Reformers without noting the remarkable amount of ink, argument, and emotion that went into the criticisms of enthusiastic religion. Many in our day who might criticize us for referring too much to the Reformers and other giants of church history are often, ironically, the same people whose theology sounds so much like Oprah Winfrey or Lee Iacocca. We all take people with us to Scripture, guides who have so influenced our understanding of biblical teaching that we do not often realize the extent to which our reading of Scripture is informed and, perhaps, deformed by our dependence on them. Like the defendant who cannot afford a lawyer, the court of public opinion will provide us with our counsel unless we pay the price to find it elsewhere. Some of us go to Scripture with Ireneaus, Augustine, Anselm, Luther, Calvin, and Warfield. How can evangelicals attack the current president for ignoring *America's* heritage when they so often dismiss the wisdom of the *church's* founding fathers and reformers? C. S. Lewis called the modern attitude toward the past "chronological snobbery."

We have creeds, confessions, and catechisms not because we want to arrogantly assert ourselves above Scripture or other Christians, but for precisely the opposite reason: We are convinced that such self-assertion is actually easiest for us when we presume to be going to Scripture alone and directly, without any presuppositions or expectations. With Isaiah, I must confess, "I am a man of unclean lips and I dwell among a people of unclean lips." As if my own ignorance and folly were not enough, I belong by divine providence to one of the most superficial, banal, and ungodly generations in history and am bound to be negatively shaped by my context in ways that are different from other saints in other times and places. Fearful of our own weaknesses in judgment and blind spots due to our own acculturation, we go to Scripture with the wider church, with those who have confessed the same faith for centuries.

Nobody goes to the Bible alone, but carries with him or her a host of influences. It is infinitely easier to distort the Word of God when we cut ourselves off from the consensus of other Christians across time and place. Just as the Reformers criticized medieval theologians as "Sophists"—the nasty nickname for wishy-washy relativists who never met a compromise they didn't like—we, too, are faced by a growing dissatisfaction with making clear and precise theological statements. We may despair of the detailed arguments and refined systems of the past that occupied our forebears, but we ignore them at our own peril and that of our children.

Third, in order to recover the sufficiency of Scripture we must once again learn to distinguish the Law and the gospel as the "two words" of Scripture.

For the Reformers, it was not enough to believe in inerrancy. Since Rome also had a high view of Scripture in theory, the Reformers were not criticizing the church for denying its divine character. Rather, they argued that Rome subverted its high view of Scripture by the addition of other words and by failing to read and proclaim Scripture according to its most obvious sense.

At the heart of the movement's hermeneutics was the distinction between "Law" and "gospel." For the Reformers, this was not equivalent to "Old Testament" and "New Testament," respectively; rather, it meant, in the words of Theodore Beza, "We divide this Word into two principal parts or kinds: the one is called the 'Law,' the other the 'Gospel.' For all the rest can be gathered under the one or other of these two headings." The Law "is written by nature in our hearts," while "What we call the Gospel (Good News) is a doctrine which is not at all in us by nature, but which is revealed from Heaven (Mt. 16:17; John 1:13)." The Law leads us to Christ in the gospel by condemning us and causing us to despair of our own "righteousness." "Ignorance of this distinction between Law and Gospel," Beza wrote, "is one of the principal sources of the abuses which corrupted and still corrupt Christianity."[11]

Luther made this hermeneutic central, but both traditions of the Protestant Reformation jointly affirm this key distinction. In much of medieval preaching, the Law and gospel were so confused that the "Good News" seemed to be that Jesus was a "kinder, gentler Moses," who softened the Law into easier exhortations, such as loving God and neighbor from the heart. The Reformers saw Rome as teaching that the gospel was simply an easier "law" than that of the Old Testament. Instead of following a lot of rules, God expects only love and heartfelt surrender. Calvin replied, "As if we could think of anything more difficult than to love God with all our heart, all our soul, and all our strength! Compared with this law, everything could be considered easy. . . . [For] the law cannot do anything else than to accuse and blame all to a man, to convict, and, as it were, apprehend them; in fine, to condemn them in God's judgment: that God alone may justify, that all flesh may keep silence before him."[12] Thus, Calvin observes, Rome could only see the gospel as that which enables believers to become righteous by obedience and that which is "a compensation for their lack," not realizing that the Law requires perfection, not approximation.[13]

Of course, no one claims to have arrived at perfection, and yet, Calvin says, many do claim "to have yielded completely to God, [claiming that] they have kept the law in part and are, in respect to this part, righteous."[14] Only the terror of the Law can shake us of this self-confidence. Thus, the Law condemns and drives us to Christ, so that the gospel can comfort without any threats or exhortations that might lead to doubt. In one of his earliest writings, Calvin defended this evangelical distinction between Law and gospel:

> All this will readily be understood by describing the Law and describing the Gospel and then comparing them. Therefore, the Gospel is the message, the salvation-bringing proclamation concerning Christ that he was sent by God the Father . . . to procure eternal life. The Law is contained in precepts, it threatens, it burdens, it promises no goodwill. The Gospel acts without threats, it does not drive one on by precepts, but rather teaches us about the supreme goodwill of God towards us. Let whoever therefore is desirous of having a plain and honest understanding of the Gospel, test everything by the above descriptions of the Law and the Gospel. Those who do not follow this method of treatment will never be adequately versed in the Philosophy of Christ.[15]

While the Law continues to guide the believer in the Christian life, Calvin insists that it can never be confused with the Good News. Even *after* conversion, believers are in desperate need of the gospel because they read the commands, exhortations, threats, and warnings of the Law and often waver in their certain confidence because they do not see in themselves this righteousness that is required. Am I *really* surrendered? Have I *truly* yielded in every area of my life? What if I have not experienced the same things that other Christians regard as normative? Do I really possess the Holy Spirit? What if I fall into serious sin? These are questions that we all face in pastoral ministry, as in our own lives. What will restore our peace and hope in the face of such questions? The Reformers, with the prophets and apostles, were convinced that only the gospel could bring such comfort to struggling Christians.

Without this constant emphasis in preaching, we can never truly worship or serve God in liberty, our gaze fastened on ourselves in either despair or self-righteousness, rather than on Christ. Law and gospel must both ever be preached, both for conviction and instruction, but the conscience will never rest, Calvin says, so long as gospel is mixed with Law. "Consequently, this Gospel does not impose any commands, but rather reveals God's goodness, his mercy and his benefits."[16] This distinction, Calvin says with Luther and the other Reformers, marks the difference between Christianity and paganism: "All who deny this turn the whole of the Gospel upside down; they utterly bury Christ, and destroy all true worship of God."[17]

Ursinus, primary author of the Heidelberg Catechism, said that the Law–gospel distinction has "comprehended the sum and substance of the sacred Scriptures," are "the chief and general divisions of the holy scriptures, and comprise the entire doctrine comprehended therein."[18] To confuse them is to corrupt the faith at its core.[19] While the Law must be preached as divine instruction for the Christian life, it must never be used to shake believers from the confidence that Christ is their "righteousness, holiness and redemption" (1 Cor. 1:30). The believer goes to the Law and loves that Law for its divine wisdom, for it reveals the will of the One to whom we are now reconciled by the gospel. But the believer cannot find pardon, mercy, victory, or even the power to obey it, by going to the Law itself any more *after* conversion than before. It is still always the Law that commands and the gospel that gives. This is why every sermon must be carefully crafted on this foundational distinction.

As he watched the Baptist Church in England give way to moralism in the so-called Down-grade Controversy, Charles Spurgeon declared, "There is no point on which men make greater mistakes than on the relation which exists between the law and the gospel. Some men put the law instead of the gospel; others put gospel

1 Co 1:30

instead of the law. A certain class maintains that the law and the gospel are mixed. . . . These men understand not the truth and are false teachers."[20]

In our day, these categories are once again confused in even the most conservative churches. Even where the categories of psychology, marketing, and politics do not replace those of Law and gospel, much of evangelical preaching today softens the Law and confuses the gospel with exhortations, often leaving people with the impression that God does not expect the perfect righteousness prescribed in the Law, but a generally good heart and attitude and avoidance of major sins. A gentle moralism prevails in much of evangelical preaching today, and one rarely hears the Law preached as God's condemnation and wrath, but as helpful suggestions for a more fulfilled life. In the place of God's Law, helpful tips for practical living are often offered. (In one large conservative church in which I preached recently, the sermon was identified in the program as "Lifestyle Perspectives." Only occasionally was one reminded that it was a church service and not a Rotary meeting.) The piety and faith of the biblical characters are often preached as examples to imitate, along with Thomas Jefferson and Benjamin Franklin. As in Protestant liberalism, such preaching often fails to hold Christ forth as the divine Savior of sinners, but instead presents him as the coach whose play-book will show us how to achieve victory.

Sometimes it is due less to conviction than to a lack of precision. For instance, we often hear calls to "live the gospel," and yet nowhere in Scripture are we called to "live the gospel." Instead, we are told to *believe* the gospel and *obey* the Law, receiving God's favor from the one and God's guidance from the other. The gospel—or Good News—is not that God will help us achieve his favor with his help, but that someone *else* lived the *Law* in our place and fulfilled all righteousness. Others confuse the Law and gospel by replacing the demands of the Law with the simple command to "surrender all" or "make Jesus Lord and Savior," as if this one little work secured eternal life. J. Gresham Machen, earlier this century, declared, "According to modern liberalism, faith is essentially the same as 'making Christ master' of one's life. . . . But that simply means that salvation is thought to be obtained by our obedience to the commands of Christ. Such teaching is just a sublimated form of legalism."[21] In another work, Machen added,

> What good does it do to me to tell me that the type of religion presented in the Bible is a very fine type of religion and that the thing for me to do is just to start practicing that type of religion now? . . . I will tell you, my friend. It does me not one tiniest little bit of good. . . . What I need first of all is not exhortation, but a gospel, not directions for saving myself but knowledge of how God has saved me. Have you any good news? That is the question that I ask of you. I know your exhortations will not help me. But if anything has been done to save me, will you not tell me the facts?[22]

Does that mean that the Word of God does not command our obedience or that such obedience is optional? Certainly not! But it does mean that obedience must not be confused with the gospel. Our best obedience is corrupted, so how could that be good news? The gospel is that Christ was crucified for our sins and was raised for our justification. The gospel *produces* new life, new experiences, and a new obedience, but too often we confuse the fruit or effects with the gospel itself. Nothing that happens *within us* is, properly speaking, "gospel," but it is the gospel's effect. Paul instructs us, "conduct yourselves in a manner worthy of the gospel of Christ" (Phil. 1:27). While the gospel contains no commands or threats, the Law indeed does, and the Christian is still obligated to both "words" he or she hears from the mouth of God. Like the Godhead or the two natures of Christ, we must neither divorce nor confuse Law and gospel.

When the Law is softened into gentle promises and the gospel is hardened into conditions and exhortations, believers often find themselves in a deplorable state. For those who know their own hearts, preaching that tries to tone down the Law by assuring them that God looks on the heart comes as bad news, not good news: "The heart is deceitful above all things" (Jer. 17:9). Many Christians have experienced the confusion of Law and gospel in their diet, where the gospel was free and unconditional when they became believers, but is now pushed into the background to make room for an almost exclusive emphasis on exhortations. Again, it is not that exhortations do not have their place, but they must never be confused with the gospel and that gospel of divine forgiveness is as important for sinful believers to hear as it is for unbelievers. Nor can we assume that believers ever progress beyond the stage where they need to hear the gospel, as if the Good News ended at conversion. For, as Calvin said, "We are all partly unbelievers throughout our lives." We must constantly hear God's promise in order to counter the doubts and fears that are natural to us.

But there are many, especially in our narcissistic age, whose ignorance of the Law leads them into a carnal security. Thus, people often conclude that they are "safe and secure from all alarm" because they walked an aisle, prayed a prayer, or signed a card, even though they have never had to give up their own fig leaves in order to be clothed with the righteousness of the Lamb of God. Or perhaps, although they have not perfectly loved God and neighbor, they conclude that they are at least "yielded," "surrendered," or "letting the Spirit have his way"; that they are "living in victory over all known sin" and enjoying the "higher life." Deluding themselves and others, they need to be stripped of their fig leaves in order to be clothed with the skins of the Lamb of God. Thus, Machen writes,

> A new and more powerful proclamation of law is perhaps the most pressing need of the hour; men would have little difficulty with the gospel if they had only learned the lesson of the law. As it is, they are turning aside from the Christian pathway; they are turning to the village of Morality, and to the house of Mr. Legality, who is reported to be very skillful in relieving men of their burdens. . . . 'Making Christ Master' in the life, putting into practice 'the principles of Christ' by one's own efforts—these are merely new ways of earning salvation by one's obedience to God's commands. And they are undertaken because of a lax view of what those commands are. So it always is: a low view of law always brings legalism in religion; a high view of law makes a man a seeker after grace.[23]

We must, therefore, recover Law and gospel, and with such preaching, the Christocentric message of Scripture, or no good will come of our work, regardless of how committed we are to inerrancy.

We cannot say that we are preaching the Word of God unless we are distinctly and clearly proclaiming both God's judgment and his justification as the regular diet in our congregations. To recover Scripture's sufficiency we must, therefore, like the Reformers, recover the distinctions between things heavenly and things earthly, between God's inscripturated Word and individual enthusiasm, and between Law and gospel. This leads directly to the second *"sola."*

Solus Christus

To say that the point of the Bible is redemptive is to say that Christ is the central figure. Only by defending Scripture alone are we certain that the church will cling to Christ alone. Audaciously, Jesus accused the biblical scholars of his day of not knowing the Scriptures (Matt. 2:29; Luke 24:45) and declared, "You diligently study the Scriptures because you think that by them you possess eternal life. These are the Scriptures that testify about me, yet you refuse to come to me to have life" (John 5:39). After his resurrection, our Lord explained the Scriptures on the Emmaus road to two of his followers. But first, he sharply rebuked them for failing to read the Old Testament with himself at the center: "'How foolish you are, and how slow of heart to believe all that the prophets have spoken!' . . . And beginning with Moses and all the Prophets, he explained to them what was said in all the Scriptures concerning himself" (Luke 24:27). Imagine the power of *that* sermon! No wonder their hearts burned within them! Jesus here teaches us how we are to read and preach the Bible. It is not chiefly about Bible heroes or lessons in life, but the revelation of Christ. Similarly, Peter reminds us that the chief message of the entire Old Testament is "the sufferings of Christ and the glories that would follow" (1 Peter 1:11).

As we have noted, the Law is written on our conscience in creation and everyone knows right from wrong. In fact, if one is looking primarily for a book of stories designed to teach a moral lesson, the Bible may not be as good as Aesop's Fables. All of the biblical heroes represent sinfulness, disobedience, half-heartedness, and pride as well as faith and obedience. The real hero is God, who remains faithful to his promise in spite of human sin. No moral instruction comes easily to us, but the gospel is not in us by nature; it must be revealed from heaven. This is chiefly why we have the Word of God.

To preach the Bible as "the handbook for life" or as the answer to every question, rather than as the revelation of Christ, is to turn the Bible into an entirely different book. This is how the Pharisees approached Scripture, however, as we can see clearly from the questions they asked Jesus, all of them amounting to something akin to Trivial Pursuits: "What happens if a person divorces and remarries?" "Why do your disciples pick grain on the Sabbath?" "Who sinned—this man or his parents—that he was born blind?" For the Pharisees, the Scriptures were a source of trivia for life's dilemmas. To be sure, Scripture provides God-centered and divinely revealed wisdom for life, but if this were its primary objective, Christianity would be a religion of self-improvement by following examples and exhortations, not a religion of the cross. This is Paul's point with the Corinthians, whose obsession with wisdom and miracles had obscured the true wisdom and the greatest miracle of all. And what is that? "He has been made for us our righteousness, holiness, and redemption," Paul replies (1 Cor. 1:28–31).

In popular culture, entertainers, speech-writers, teachers, writers of television situation comedies and movies don't know exactly how they should portray a minister, but what almost always comes out is a guy who helps us figure out whether we should pay extra for not rewinding the video before we return it. In these representations, the minister is there to help us with our ethical dilemmas, but the possibility of something uniquely Christian falling from his lips would be inconceivable. Is this all caricature? Is there not something to the sense that many people have that, for the most part, religion has to do with how we cope with life here and now rather than ultimate questions of truth and eternity? Philosopher William James said that the test of a particular truth-claim is "its cash-value in experiential terms." The big question, says James, is, "Will it work?" A contemporary follower of James, Richard Rorty, argues that the only criterion for judging truth-claims is their therapeutic usefulness. Now, we might cringe at the naked celebration of narcissistic relativism, but this is too often the way evangelicals argue for a "felt needs" approach to evangelism and worship today, like the liberal Protestants before them. Like the Pharisees, we very often read and use Scripture as a catalogue of helpful hints—in other words, as either politics or therapy. Very often, an emphasis on the believer's "personal testimony" pushes Christ aside. Again Machen observes,

> Christian evangelism does not consist merely in a man going about the world saying, "Look at me, what a wonderful experience I have, how happy I am, what wonderful Christian virtues I exhibit; you can all be as good and as happy as I am if you will just make a complete surrender of your wills in obedience to what I say." . . . Men are not saved by the exhibition of our glorious Christian virtues; they are not saved by the contagion of our experiences. . . . Nay, we must preach to them the Lord Jesus Christ; for it is only through the gospel which sets him forth that they can be saved. If you want health for your souls, and if you want to be the instruments of bringing health to others, do not turn your gaze forever within, as though you could find Christ there. Nay, turn your gaze away from your own miserable experiences, away from your own sin, to the Lord Jesus Christ as he is offered to us in the gospel.[24]

Like Niebuhr later, Machen was criticizing liberalism that was just then the juice of pietism turning into the vinegar of apostasy. Today's pietism is tomorrow's liberalism. Similarly, the Reformers believed that Rome had obscured Christ in a number of ways. It was not only due to sacerdotalism or the cult of the Virgin, saints, and martyrs, but had much to do with the fact that the theology of the Middle Ages was human-centered. That is not to say that it did not have its God-centered elements, but these were subordinate. Largely on the basis of Paul's Epistles, Luther especially contrasted the theology of glory and the theology of the cross. According to the former path, seekers climbed ladders of merit, speculation, and mysticism to experience God directly. The theology of the cross was offensive because its focus was on God and his saving action in Christ, not on man and his spiritual ascent through self-effort, worldly wisdom, and exciting experiences. All of these were attempts, in Luther's words, to see God in the nude, to experience him directly apart from Christ.

Like the Corinthians, many modern evangelicals are obsessed with either practical wisdom or signs and wonders, and with these concerns made central, the preaching, the worship, and the outreach all find the cross offensive or oddly out of place. Contrast the cross-centered hymns, for instance, of Isaac Watts, Charles Wesley, and Augustus Toplady with today's most popular praise songs in which sentimentalism seems to be the key note. Where is the cross? It is lost in a theology of glory, a message of triumphalism leading to burnout, instead of despair leading to Christ.

Therefore, Christ is increasingly championed within popular evangelicalism as primarily a moral example who most sublimely illustrates God's love and forgiveness and gives us helpful guidelines more than a substitutionary sacrifice for sinners who deserve divine wrath.

In short, to preach Christ is specifically to proclaim him in his offices as Prophet, Priest, and King. We need no other prophets to reveal God's Word or will; no further priest to mediate divine salvation and blessing; and no additional king to rule the doctrine and life of churches or individual Christians. And further, to represent Christ chiefly as the Divine Therapist, Guide, Lover, Hero, Power-Source, Political Reformer, Healer, Coach, or anything else other than the Mediator between God and the wicked is to remove the centrality of Christ by undercutting the centrality of his genuine mission and office (1 Cor. 1:22–2:2).

The insidious nature of "truth-decay" is seen in the subtle ways in which the centrality of Christ and his mediatorial work is undercut, but once Christ's priestly office is obscured, it is easier to erect more direct obstacles. For instance, in the arguments often made for benignly innocuous ("non-sectarian") prayer in public schools or in the civic prayers that are often offered in meetings sponsored by people of mixed religious commitments, the assumption is that genuine access to "God" may be achieved apart from either a proper object (the Triune God) or a proper Mediator. As one evangelical respondent in a recent survey declared, "We all access God differently." While we have heard much about the politics of civil prayer, where are the theological objections being raised? Even more disconcerting than the subtleties of civil religion are the findings of James D. Hunter, George Gallup, and George Barna in this regard. According to recent studies, 35 percent of America's evangelical seminarians deny that faith in Christ is absolutely necessary and the same percentage of the entire adult evangelical population agrees: "God will save all good people when they die, regardless of whether they've trusted in Christ."[25] Of course, the last statistic rests on the premise, widely plausible to our society, that human beings are basically good, which receives an approving nod from 77 percent of America's evangelicals,[26] and that leads us to the next Reformation slogan: "Grace Alone."

Sola Gratia

If human beings are basically good and evil is attributable to impersonal forces, structures, institutions, and upbringing, the doctrine of grace—the essence of the gospel—is meaningless. For centuries, this has been called Pelagianism, but today it is embraced by the clear majority of evangelicals. This demonstrates the extent to which secularism dominates the belief-structures of many who claim to be orthodox "Bible believers."

Although some medieval church leaders warned against a creeping Pelagianism (most notably, Thomas Bradwardine, fourteenth-century archbishop of Canterbury, and Johann von Staupitz, Luther's superior in the Augustinian Order), the Reformers themselves did not accuse the church of this heresy because the official teaching of the magisterium condemned it for its weak views of sin and grace. What the Reformers did condemn was Semi-Pelagianism, which was captured in the slogan, *facienti quod in se est Deus non denegat gratiam* ("God will not deny his grace to those who do that which lies within their power"). Grace, in the medieval mind, was akin to a substance that was infused or poured into believers in order to transform them as they cooperated with it. The average believer could draw upon this grace, but the truly devoted could secure it by extraordinary zeal and spiritual techniques. Once again, the

Reformers charged that this manifested an anthropocentric theology that had not really come to terms with St. Anselm's warning, "You have not yet considered how great your sin is."

✶S

Once again in our day the weakening of our doctrine of sin and the waning awareness of despair in preaching, teaching, and publishing have led to an insufficient view of grace. If one feels utterly condemned and helpless, a gospel that proclaims divine grace as forgiveness is the undoubted answer, but if one feels merely wayward, unhappy, unfulfilled, and weak, a gospel that offers infused assistance is quite sufficient. The modern equivalent of "God will not deny his grace to those who do that which lies within their power" might be, "God helps those who help themselves," the latter endorsed by 87 percent of American evangelicals, that number rising with frequency of involvement in evangelical churches.[27] But all too often it is secular writers who raise these questions, as in *Newsweek*'s recent article whose title repeated that of a secular psychologist: "Whatever Became of Sin?" In this article, the author says that the whole notion of guilt has been dismissed "in the current upbeat mood of American religion."[28]

How did we come to this pass? Is it simply that we are coming belatedly to the conclusions championed earlier this century by the modernists, or are the seeds of destruction sown earlier than this century? Sadly, both liberalism and evangelicalism may arguably share the same parentage in frontier revivalism. Much of American revivalism is responsible for a Pelagian renaissance even before the arrival of Protestant liberalism. It was not Feuerbach, but Finney, who declared, "There is nothing in religion beyond the ordinary powers of nature. It consists entirely in the right exercise of the powers of nature. It is just that and nothing else. When mankind become religious, they are not *enabled* to put forth exertions which they were unable before to put forth. They only exert powers which they had before, in a different way, and use them for the glory of God." So, for Finney, even revival—the corporate conversion of sinners—is "not a miracle, nor dependent on a miracle, in any sense. It is a purely philosophical result of the right use of the constituted means—as much so as any other effect produced by the application of means." This meant, said Finney, that the evangelist could

HERE HERE!
(British >>emeny)

Finney⟶ Soli Deo Gloria

only be successful by employing "powerful excitements."[29] It must be conceded, in all fairness to Rome, that Finney's convictions would have been condemned not only by the Reformers, but by the Roman Catholic magisterium as a denial of the biblical doctrines of sin and grace. Evangelicalism has inherited this pragmatic and naturalistic tendency of America's Counter-Reformation, so that when one of today's evangelical theologians declares that "we have finally made peace with the culture of modernity,"[30] it is not simply the capitulation of conservatives to liberalism but of Protestants generally to an incipient Pelagianism that has been present in revivalism since the beginning of the nineteenth century. Ironically, many conservative Christians who decry naturalism in the wider culture, especially in science, nevertheless imitate Finney's religious naturalism in evangelism, worship, and politics.

Right on!

To say that salvation is by grace alone is not only to affirm the supernatural character of salvation, but is to exclude any form of synergism (i.e., salvation as the result of human–divine cooperation). While the new birth brings about a new obedience in which one begins to cooperate with God in his or her growth, human decision and effort are strictly excluded as playing any role in our new birth: "It does not, therefore, depend on man's desire or effort, but on God's mercy" (Rom. 9:16).

The Reformation insisted upon this theocentric conception, exalting divine election against free will and divine descent against human ascent in all of its forms. We are reminded of Luther's heated exchange with Erasmus under the unambiguous title, *The Bondage of the Will*. While we may differ on other related beliefs, those who are convinced that the Reformation was essentially on the mark are not given the luxury of not taking a stand on unconditional election and the monergistic work of the Holy Spirit in granting new life. Therefore, if we are really convinced of the justice in the Reformation's critique of medieval Rome, we can no longer fail to regard Arminianism within Protestant circles as any more acceptable. It is not only Rome, but the Wesleyan system, especially as it is mediated through Charles Finney, Pentecostalism and the revivalist tradition, which must be equally rejected to the extent that each fails to sufficiently honor God's grace. To the extent that Protestantism exalted man at God's expense, to that extent it accommodated to the modern age and this is, no doubt, at the heart of the crisis that has brought us here, to repent, recover, and confess.

This recovery about which we are speaking is a difficult task that requires us to arrive at conclusions that may deprive us of peace and honor in our current positions. Of all our efforts, this will be the most difficult. After all, in our cafeteria approach to truth, Americans will happily embrace everything we say and then place a saucer of Toronto Blessing and a plate of political ideology on the tray as well, chased perhaps by a glass of self-esteem therapy. We must engage in antithesis. We must declare, with the Reformers and with the Athanasian Creed, not only, "We believe . . . ," but, "Therefore, we condemn. . . ." We must not only clearly state our arguments, but be willing to articulate which opposing beliefs and practices will therefore not be consistent.

On no other truth is this "antithesis" more important than "grace alone." Paul employed just this sort of antithesis when he declared, "If then election is by grace, it is not of works. Otherwise grace is no longer grace" (Rom. 11:6). This is the sort of clarity we desperately need in this hour. This theocentric emphasis undergirding the theology of the Reformation has been called the "Copernican Revolution" in church history, and while the Roman Catholic Counter-Reformation occurred in the late sixteenth century, the Protestant Counter-Reformation has been successful for the past two centuries. Defending *sola gratia* in our age will certainly be no less difficult for us than it was for the Reformers, and it leads us to the next *"sola."*

Sola Fide

If all of salvation is due to divine graciousness, the gospel of free justification comes into sharper focus.

It is "the article by which the church stands or falls," Luther and Calvin declared of "faith alone." As the medieval church did not deny the authority of Scripture, or the need for Christ and grace, so it did not deny the importance of faith. In fact, there could be no salvation apart from it, the medieval church insisted. But faith was viewed merely as formal assent to the teaching of the church. The Reformers noticed that throughout Scripture faith was described as a matter not only of knowledge and assent, but also of trust—relying on God's promise in Christ to save sinners. Because of its view of faith, the medieval church concluded that something else was required in order for faith to be truly saving, so love was viewed as the formal additive that shaped and brought faith to completion. In this way, one could even speak of justification by faith, but this meant sanctification by cooperation with infused grace. In baptism, God infused initial grace into the believer so that the *habitus* or "nature" of new life would be implanted.

The Reformers realized that this owed more to Aristotle than to Scripture. Furthermore, Luther himself was in debt to the noted Renaissance humanist Erasmus for discovering discrepancies between the Latin Vulgate (Jerome's translation upon which the church had depended) and the Greek New Testament. The most glaring, at least from Luther's point of view, was the erroneous translation of the Greek word "to justify." The original Greek word, *diakaiosune,* which means "to *declare* righteous," was instead translated with the Latin verb *iustificare,* which means "to *make* righteous." Thus, justification was seen as a process of becoming or being made righteous rather than a declarative act in a courtroom.

This Vulgate translation had led Luther, along with the rest of the medieval world, to believe that salvation consisted in cooperating with God's grace as one was transformed into a righteous person. In other words, justification and sanctification were one and the same. Before, Luther had read of God's righteousness in terms of something that God demanded, but now he realized—especially in the light of Romans and Galatians—that it was also a righteousness that God gave. And not only was it given as an infused *habitus,* but as a gift of right standing. In other words, Luther finally realized that justification was a legal, not a moral, change.

God demands a perfect righteousness, said Luther. No, just a willingness to cooperate with grace, said Rome. But Luther was led even by Rome's own Greek scholars to recognize the Bible's clarity on the objective, forensic character of justification and realized that the only perfect righteousness is Christ's. Luther was finally convinced that the Scriptures clearly taught two essential things: God cannot accept imperfect righteousness, and therefore he imputes (credits) to the believer the "alien righteousness" of Christ, which is perfect. Thus, the believer is *simul iustus et peccator*—"simultaneously justified and yet sinful." Although sanctification (God's work within believers) is incomplete in this life and believers always have reason to be judged because of their own wickedness, they are not judged because the perfect righteousness of Christ is credited to them through faith alone. The Reformation's way of putting it was, *per fidem propter Christum*—by faith, because of Christ. They put it this way so that people would not view faith as the basis for justification, since it is easy to turn faith into the "one small work" that earned justification. Christ, not faith, is valuable and inexhaustible in riches of righteousness. Even faith is mingled with doubt and often weak, but it is the strength of Christ's righteousness, not of the believer's faith, that keeps one in a right standing before God.

In our day, the doctrine of justification is widely ignored, rarely central, and not infrequently denied outright by Protestant—tragically, even evangelical—theologians and pastors. If the statistics cited above are in any way indicative of reality, 87 percent of America's evangelicals are practicing medieval Roman Catholics in their view of how one relates to God. Very often, the emphasis falls on the work of Christ or the Holy Spirit within the believer for achieving "the victorious Christian life," or on steps and principles of getting close to God. In the midst of our subjective emphasis on the inner life, how desperately we need to hear Luther's famous counsel to Melanchthon: "The gospel lies entirely outside of you!"

The medieval church feared that these views would lead to the conclusion that one need not be troubled about obedience and love if he or she was already declared righteous the moment of belief. That, too, seems to trouble many modern evangelicals. This goes deep into our recent history, with Pietism's emphasis on the inner life and Wesley's impatience at certain points in his ministry with the doctrine of forensic justification. In spite of the vast differences, all the major religious expressions in America, liberal or conservative, New Age or evangelical, share at least one thing in common: They are, to varying degrees, inward and subjective in their orientation.

We have already seen how deeply committed Charles Finney was to Pelagian convictions. We should, therefore, not be surprised to find him rejecting *sola fide* as well, boldly declaring that this doctrine, like original sin and the substitutionary atonement, was "impossible and absurd."[31] Finney writes, "As has been already said, there can be no justification in a legal or forensic sense, but upon the ground of universal, perfect, and uninterrupted obedience to law. . . . The doctrine of an imputed righteousness, or that Christ's obedience to the law was accounted as our obedience, is founded on a most false and nonsensical assumption," that assumption being the substitutionary atonement. "The doctrine of an imputed righteousness," he said, "is a different gospel,"[32] and the revivalistic tradition generally tended to stress human activity sometimes even more dangerously than Rome had articulated. At least Rome made Christ the principal ground of justification and denied the possibility that believers could attain moral perfection, much less be justified thereby.

Our evangelical tradition, therefore, is at crossroads on this essential point as well. Fuller Seminary's Russell Spittler writes, "But can it really be true—saint and sinner simultaneously? I wish it were so. . . . Is this correct: 'I don't need to work at *becoming*. I'm already declared to be holy.' No sweat needed? It looks wrong to me. I hear moral demands in Scripture. . . . Still, I'm grateful for Luther's phrase and for his descendants. . . . But *simul iustus et peccator?* I hope it's true! I simply fear it's not."[33]

Clark Pinnock is so uncomfortable with an objective justification that he favors "the possibility of a doctrine of purgatory." He says, "Our Wesleyan and Arminian thinking may need to be extended in this direction."[34] This is not to suggest that such eccentric comments would be endorsed by a significant majority of evangelicals, but it is to suggest that the so-called evangelical megashift described by *Christianity Today* in 1990 (February 19) is drawing deeply on the incipient Pelagianism within American Protestantism and the modern consciousness. This megashift includes a "new-model" evangelicalism that is critical of preaching that is concerned with divine wrath, original and personal sin, a vicarious atonement, and forensic justification.[35] Insufficiently "relational" and sensitive to the experiences of contemporary men and women, the classical evangelical paradigm, we are told, tends to offend unnecessarily. The triumph of the therapeutic within evangelicalism is acutely illustrated in Ray Anderson's warning: "If our sin is viewed as causing the death of Jesus on the cross, then we ourselves become victims of a 'psychological battering' produced by the cross. When I am led to feel that the pain and torment of Jesus' death on the cross is due to my sin, I inflict upon myself spiritual and psychological torment."[36]

Should we view such comments as exceptional departures that should not be used to reflect the general state of evangelicalism? Surely many evangelical pastors would feel awkward in making such bold statements, but the point here worth making is that these sentiments differ in degree, but not in kind, from the diet that is typical of evangelical preaching, publishing, and broadcasting in our day. In other words, the aspects of the modern consciousness that make the relational a dominant category and drive classical motifs to the periphery of vision are so widespread that the most conservative evangelicals find themselves sympathetic to the "new model" evangelicals for reasons they often feel but do not understand. Even if they refuse to "revision" evangelical theology, more conservative evangelicals now implicitly share the same worldview and in practice often follow assumptions that they might deny if directly put to them. Thus, it is essential that we not only wait for signs of actual apostasy or explicit departures, but that we get beneath the most egregious declarations in an attempt to discern the larger story of modern consciousness.

While the entire revivalistic tradition cannot be condemned as explicitly Pelagian, it has tended to confuse these issues considerably, at least in its more popular forms. Challenges to the Reformation's doctrine of *sola fide* have come from every quarter: biblical theology, systematic theology, Old and New Testament faculties, parachurch leaders, and evangelists. But most of the time, it is neither affirmed nor denied, but ignored. To the extent that the church is driven by the felt needs of the culture, salvation from divine wrath and justification before a holy God will be "foolishness to those who are perishing." In 1993 *Newsweek* ran a story on a megachurch in Arizona that had traded in catechesis and preaching for "Steven Spielberg-like Sunday school gimmicks [and] the generic Amy Grant music at worship service" as well as drama in place of a sermon. The church's pastor told *Newsweek,* "People today aren't interested in traditional doctrines like justification, sanctification, and redemption."[37] But if such apostolic truths are not as relevant as, say, relief from stress or happier marriages, what does that tell us? It tells us what *is,* but not what *ought to be.*

It is precisely because justification is *not* the unbeliever's "felt need" that we must preach the Law. Suddenly even religious people who thought they were gaining victory sense the depth of their depravity as they cry out with the publican, "Lord, be merciful to me, a sinner!" The need for mercy is only felt after the reality of guilt makes its impression. Only then can the gospel relieve. If the gospel is no longer relevant, we do not change our message in order to be more "practical"; we make sure that we are preaching the Law in its strict terror, followed by the warm-hearted announcement of the peace God has made by his Son's blood, received through faith alone. Why *should* unchurched Harry and Mary have the felt need for Christ's righteousness if they are not aware of their nakedness before a holy God? When we are told that the message of divine wrath and holiness will not appeal to the seekers of our day, that is hardly surprising news! The cry for grace will never be appealing until there is a sense of guilt and despair once more in our churches.

If this doctrine, the recovery of which has always been at the bottom of every major awakening in church history, is the truth by which the church stands or falls—if, in other words, it is nothing less than the gospel itself—there can be no doubt that the decay of the contemporary church is due in no small measure to the slighting of this central tenet. It is meant not only to be affirmed as part of a confessional subscription, but to be proclaimed as the "good news" that justifies not only the believer before God but justifies the existence of the church in the world.

Soli Deo Gloria

The current pope signs his letters, "To The Greater Glory of God," and there is no doubt that Roman Catholicism has had a place in its theology for God's glory. But like the other themes we have mentioned, it was just a place in a theological system that had more important doctrines to which these themes were subordinate. To say that Rome was human-centered is not to suggest that the God-centered element was entirely missing, but it is to say that the latter was subordinate to the former. If human beings contributed to their own salvation in any way, either by "willing or running," as Paul puts it, or if salvation is conceived eudaemonistically as a means *def* to happiness in this life rather than reconciliation with a holy God, the unquestionable result is an anthropocentric religion.

x s

Reconciliation with God is not a means to a greater end of self-fulfillment, therapeutic well-being, or even moral virtue. Reconciliation with God is a legitimate end in itself; it is the realization of God's glory in the redemption of sinners and it does not need something higher than that to justify its importance. To preach Scripture is to preach Christ; to preach Christ is to preach the cross; to preach the cross is to preach grace; to preach grace is to preach justification; to preach justification is to attribute all of salvation to the glory of God and to respond to that Good News in grateful obedience through one's vocation in the world.

Luther took pains to distinguish his work from earlier "reformations." Not unlike many of the frenetic movements of reform, renewal, and revival in our day, the others were concerned with morals, church life, and structural changes, but said Luther, "We took aim at the doctrine." It was not that these other areas were unimportant, but that they were proximate in their importance. And yet, with that "Copernican Revolution," a theocentric movement was born that had enormous effects in the wider culture. The God-centered orientation of life and thought began in worship, where the focus was on God's action in Word and sacrament, instead of dazzling and entertaining the people with extravagant pageants. As believers were centered around God and his saving work in Christ, their worship services adjusted their perspective from that of a worldling to that of a redeemed sinner whose life could only have one purpose: "to glorify God and to enjoy him forever."

One thinks of J. S. Bach's signature on his compositions and carved into the organ at Leipzig *(Soli Deo Gloria)*, or of the work of

Rembrandt and the Dutch Baroque, or of the "Golden Age" of English literature, with Spenser, Milton, Herbert, Donne, and Bunyan. The rise of modern science is often attributed at least in part to the Reformation, and some of the world's leading universities were either founded or restored by those who were determined to bring Reformation theology to bear on a changing world. Observers confessed their bewilderment that so many who believed that they could contribute nothing to their salvation nevertheless led a revolution of sorts in public life. Instead of merely attacking the world, they contributed positively to culture. Freed from a private, introspective piety, these Protestants shaped the sense of public duty, helped launch democratic reforms and civil rights, and gave new dignity and direction to the godly Christian home and one's secular calling in the world. It was not a "Golden Age" in truth, but it was a wiser age in many respects, one in which some of Europe's best thinkers, artists, and professionals, as well as godly parents and neighbors, were willing to die for articles of faith that are now regarded as "irrelevant" and "divisive."

Our job, as we see it, is not to simply lament the loss of confidence in God-centered Christianity, but first to understand why these truths have lost their attraction in our day and then to communicate them with passion, precision, and the power of God's Spirit for awakening and reformation. We must be concerned not merely to defend the truth for its own sake, but to sacrifice our success, ambitions, and wisdom out of love for God and our neighbor.

But, finally, we must not merely *recover,* but *confess.* Like the Reformation itself, we envision a *kerygmatic* movement—that is, one that centers on the proclamation of the apostolic message. It is not merely an exercise in nostalgia, but the bold, loving, and cheerful announcement of "good news" in this time and place. The Reformers themselves, while respectfully drawing on church tradition, sought to understand both the gospel and those unique challenges to that Word of Life in their time and place. After five centuries, much has changed in the modern world. Although it is true that whatever was true in the sixteenth century is true in the twentieth, the modern and postmodern condition must be better understood before the gospel can address our contemporaries with power and impact. We

Barmen Confession

cannot simply rest on the laurels of our bold forebears, but must take our place in God's story, determined to locate the Archemedian points where God's address and our world can be brought into vital confrontation.

Also intended in the call to "confess" is a double meaning. First, it is confession in the sense of recognizing our faults in thought, word, and deed. Too often in the recent history of evangelicalism, there has been such a fascination with success that self-criticism has not been tolerated and is often perceived as disloyal or divisive. Rather than standing outside this situation judging others, we are among those guilty of failing to carry out our Savior's charge. A serious period of self-criticism is necessary if we are to discern where we have departed from the Christian message and its implications.

Second, "to confess" refers to the corporate and liturgical act of affirming our agreement with the hope that has preserved the church since its earliest days. We are not merely individuals passing on our personal experiences, but members of Christ's historic body, declaring what has been passed down to us (1 Cor. 15:3). Jude urges believers troubled by heresy and schism to "contend for the faith that was once for all entrusted to the saints" (v. 3). Understanding the faith as a deposit—a set of beliefs that was firmly settled long ago—is essential, especially in an existential and subjective age that does not take tradition, apostolic or otherwise, seriously. Warning Timothy against the secularism that places oneself at the center of the universe, Paul urged his pupil, "Continue in what you have learned and have become convinced of, because you know those from whom you learned it, and how from infancy you have known the holy Scriptures, which are able to make you wise for salvation through faith in Christ Jesus" (2 Tim. 3:14–15).

When the Nazis captured the Evangelical Church of Germany and that body's leading pastors actually changed its name to the "Reich's Church," swearing allegiance to Hitler, a large group of dissenting churchmen who had been involved in the Young Reformation Movement formed the "Confessing Church," so-called because of their commitment to the Reformation confessions in opposition to the nationalistic creed. The Barmen Declaration was a product of this "confessing" movement, and its leaders were convinced that it was only by opposing the forces of darkness with the eternal verities of Christian truth that the church could be the church and remain faithful to its task. They located those Archemedian points where God and man were brought into direct confrontation and confessed the faith of the fathers, but in direct relation to the challenges to the gospel and God's sovereignty in that particular day. They not only studied the confessions and stood on the confessions, but *issued* their confession in the face of their own challenges.

In our day, a far more subtle Babylonian captivity of the church has taken place, as the deeply secular presuppositions of the modern world have imprisoned the thoughts and lives of many of even the most devout believers. But the gospel—known in Scripture alone, found in Christ alone, given by grace alone, received by faith alone to the glory of God alone—is still "the power of God unto salvation." We are convinced, with all of the "confessing saints" of the past and the future, that the greatest challenge the church can pose to secularism is not mystical, moral, political, pragmatic, or institutional, but the announcement of God's work. "And though this world, with devils filled, should threaten to undo us, we will not fear, for God has willed his truth to triumph through us." And as for the father of lies, "One little word shall fell him."

6

Repentance, Recovery, and Confession

Sinclair B. Ferguson

ew events in post-apostolic history are better remembered by confessing evangelicals, or apparently more honored by them, than that monumental All Saints Eve in 1517 when Martin Luther posted his Ninety-Five Theses to the door of the Castle Church at Wittenberg.

"*Apparently* more honored"? Do evangelicals in general perhaps exercise a strange kind of implicit faith with respect to these famous theses? Probably only a minority have any idea what they contained. In the immortal perspective on history expressed by *1066 and All That,* whatever Luther's theses were exactly, we assume they were "a good thing."

They were much more than "a good thing"; the truth is that they contained statements of church-shattering importance, and none more so than the first thesis. Although provoked by the indulgences peddled by Johannes Tetzel, the very first proposition that Luther offered for public debate put the ax to the root of the tree of medieval theology:

> When our Lord and Master, Jesus Christ, said "repent," he meant that the entire life of believers should be one of repentance.

From Erasmus' Greek New Testament, Luther had come to realize that the Vulgate's rendering of Matthew 4:17 by *penitentiam agite* ("do penance") completely misinterpreted Jesus' meaning. The gospel called not for an act of penance but for a radical change of mind-set and an equally deep transformation of life. Later he would write to Staupitz about this glowing discovery: "I venture to say they are wrong who make more of the act in Latin than of the change of heart in Greek."[1]

Is it not true that we have lost sight of this note that was so prominent in Reformation theology? We could well do with a Luther *redivivus* today. For a number of important reasons evangelicals need to reconsider the centrality of repentance in our thinking about the gospel, the church, and the Christian life.

The Nature of Repentance

Even for relatively well-instructed Christians today the centrality of repentance to the gospel needs to be underlined. While it is not the instrument of justification, there is—as the Westminster Confession reminds us—no salvation without it.[2]

The Scriptures have an extensive and, in places, lively vocabulary to describe repentance. In the Old Testament various metaphors are used, such as plowing and circumcising, to make its meaning both clear and vivid. On occasion there is a focus on the emotion that characterizes repentance, namely, that of grief and regret *(naham)*. But the central Hebrew verb for repent *(sub)* is one of the dozen most common verbs in the entire Old Testament. As W. L. Holladay has noted, it occurs well over one hundred times in the specific context of God's covenant dealings with his people.[3] This is especially true in the Book of Jeremiah. To repent is to return to the provisions and prescriptions of God's bond.

The verb *sub* is, interestingly, also the verb used to describe the return of God's people from geographical exile (e.g., Isa. 10:21–22), and in many ways this provides us with a helpful metaphor to understand what repentance is. Just as restoration from exile means returning geographically from the far country to the sphere where God has covenanted to fulfill his promise of blessing, so repentance from sin means returning from the far country of bondage in sin and guilt to the place where God has promised to fulfill his covenanted blessings—and all based on the promise of God's free mercy and grace (cf. Deut. 30:11).

It is, of course, precisely this Old Testament idea that Jesus turns into an entire parable of God's grace in conversion in the story of the son who showed such prodigal indifference to his father and ended up in "the far country" only for the knowledge of the supplies in his father's house to first bring him to himself and then home to his father (Luke 15:11–32).

Biblical repentance, then, is not merely a sense of regret that leaves us where it found us; it is a radical reversal that takes us back along the road of our sinful wanderings, creating in us a completely different mind-set: We come to our senses spiritually (cf. Luke 15:17). No longer is life characterized by the demand "give me" (Luke 15:12) but now by the request "make me" (cf. Luke 15:19).

It is this that lies on the surface of the New Testament's vocabulary, which rather clearly distinguishes between the emotional epiphenomena that may accompany true repentance and true repentance itself. Paul neatly expresses these two things (regret and repentance, *metamelomai* and *metanoeo*) when he speaks about the genuine godly sorrow of a repentance we need never regret (2 Cor. 7:10). Involved in this is a change of mind-set *(metanoeo)* which is accompanied by a life-long moral and spiritual turnaround *(epistrepho)*.

This twofold character of genuine biblical repentance is well captured by the way Paul uses both ideas when he speaks about the conversion of the Thessalonians, who "turned to God from idols to serve the living and true God" (1 Thess. 1:9). It is this combination and simultaneity of turning away from and turning toward that marks genuine biblical repentance. According to Paul it involves the radical crucifixion of the flesh and yet at the same time a radical reclothing with Christ (Gal. 5:24; 3:27). It leads to an ongoing putting to death of the works of the flesh and a simultaneous putting on of the graces of Christ (Col. 3:5–11, 12–17).

Herein, then, lies the importance of Luther's statement. Repentance does not merely begin the Christian life; according to Scripture the Christian life *is* repentance from beginning to end! So long as the believer is *simul justus et peccator* it can be no other way.

No doubt there is a vividness of language, a drama of presentation in Luther that is quite unique. In nailing this first thesis to the Castle Church door he simultaneously "nailed" the gospel of Christ into the heart of the church. Who could match this?

> Repentance which is occupied with thoughts of peace is hypocrisy. There must be a great earnestness about it and a deep hurt if the old man is to be put off. When lightning strikes a tree or a man, it does two things at once—it rends the tree and swiftly slays the man. But it also turns the face of the dead man and the broken branches of the tree itself toward heaven.[4]

But while Luther's vocabulary and imagery may be uniquely vivid, his emphasis on the radical and life-long character of repentance is the common testimony of the Reformers.

This can be readily documented in the post-Reformation catechisms of various traditions. From the Heidelberg Catechism (1563) to the Westminster Assembly's Shorter Catechism (1648) there is a common emphasis on the absolute necessity and centrality of repentance.

But not only is there general agreement between Lutheran and Reformed teaching on the importance of repentance. We may go further and say that there is a special thoroughness in Calvin's exposition of it. Standing on Luther's shoulders he says things that we greatly need to hear in our own time.

For Calvin, repentance is really the personal, concrete expression of divine regeneration and renewal. He defines regeneration as repentance.[5] But more than that, he provides us with a deep exegesis of what repentance is in the New Testament. It can never be separated from faith, although it should never be confused with it. It involves a threefold cord: "denial of ourselves, mortification of our flesh, and meditation on the heavenly life."[6]

This understanding of repentance means that it can never be reduced to a single act that stands alone at the beginning of the Christian life; nor can it be understood superficially and one-dimensionally. Calvin sees that true repentance arises in the context of grace and faith, and therefore in the context of union with Jesus Christ. Indeed, since its goal is the restoration of sinners into the image of Christ, by necessity it involves the outworking of our union with Christ in his death and resurrection—what Calvin calls *mortification* and *vivification*.[7]

Faith in Christ as crucified and resurrected thus leaves a stamp on the character of the whole of our lives. This union is not only the ground plan for the Christian life, but the mold by which the Christian life is shaped. He was crucified and lives; we share in his sufferings, bear around in our bodies his dying, and are conformed to his death—all in order to share in his resurrection power and to be transformed into his glory (2 Cor. 4:10–12; Phil. 3:10–11, 20–21).

Not only my life as an individual is thus repentance-shaped; this is true of the church as a whole community united to Christ by the Spirit. Repentance in the fullest sense of restoration to God is worked out both inwardly and outwardly among us. Thus, notes Calvin, "[Peter] teaches us that the government of the Church of Christ has been so divinely constituted from the beginning that the Cross has been the way to victory, death the way to life."[8] Repentance, therefore, for Calvin, *is* the Christian life.

Of course, this emphasis we find in our forefathers was set against the background of medieval theology and medieval lifestyle. But rather than render their teaching irrelevant, this context may well provide part of the key to its relevance, because we ourselves once again need to proclaim this full-orbed doctrine of repentance within an evangelical context that has begun to manifest alarming symptoms of the medieval sickness.

The Need for Repentance

While it is with a measure of biblical authority that we can stress both the nature and centrality of repentance, it is with reticence that we draw attention to what we might call the incipient medievalizing of the evangelical church. For one thing, the present author cannot claim expertise of any kind in the sociology of church history; in addition, we all ought to have a healthy suspicion of Jeremiads if they are unaccompanied by tears (cf. Jer. 9:1, 18; 14:17; Lam. 2:11).

It is important to make clear, here, that what follows are the observations of an alien resident on only some aspects of the life of Christ's church in the United States of America. It does not profess to carry the infallibility of Christ's analysis of his church in Revelation 1–3. In addition, I wish to stress two things.

First, the church situation in which I was reared, while it may have different sicknesses, is in no less serious a pathological condition.

Second, many of us have been privileged to see many, many signs of deep encouragement in the United States. Thank God there are multitudes of congregations, some very large, some small, some well-known, some obscure, where there is a serious and joyful determination to give Jesus Christ his crowned rights in faithfulness to his Word, to live in his Spirit, to worship in his name, and to love his Father. Furthermore, it is still true that without the support of Christians in the United States world missions would collapse virtually overnight.

But having said this, must we not also say that Christ has something against us (Rev. 2:4, 14, 20)?

One of our great needs is for the ability rightly to discern some of the directions in which evangelicalism is heading, or, perhaps more accurately, disintegrating. We desperately need the long-term perspective that the history of the church gives us.

Even within the period of my own Christian life, the span between my teenage years in the 1960s and my forties in the 1990s, there has been a sea-change in evangelicalism. Many "positions" that once were standard evangelical teaching are now, after only three decades, regarded as either reactionary or even prehistoric.

If we take an even longer-term view, however, we face the alarming possibility that there may already be a medieval darkness encroaching upon evangelicalism. More perplexing yet is the fact that many of its features are welcomed as though they were fresh light. But if the light within be darkness, how great is that darkness!

Can we not detect, at least as a tendency, dynamics within evangelicalism that bear resemblances to the life of the medieval church? The possibility of a new Babylonian or (more accurately, following Luther) the Pagan Captivity of the Church looms nearer than we may be able to believe.

Consider the following five features of medieval Christianity that are evident to varying degrees in contemporary evangelicalism.

1. *Repentance has increasingly been seen as a single act, severed from a life-long restoration of godliness.*

There are complex reasons for this—not all of them modern—which we cannot explore here. Nevertheless, this seems self-evident. Seeing repentance as an isolated, completed act at the beginning of the Christian life has been a staple principle of much modern evangelicalism. Sadly that evangelicalism has often despised the theology of the confessing churches. It has spawned a generation who look back upon a single act, abstracted from its consequences, as determinative of salvation. The "altar call" has replaced the sacrament of penance. Thus repentance has been divorced from genuine regeneration, and sanctification severed from justification.

More recently, some of our brethren have been involved in the so-called Lordship Salvation Controversy. This controversy has deep and sophisticated theological and historical roots—deeper perhaps than some of its participants may have realized. But there is little doubt what a Martin Luther or a John Calvin would make of it: The idea that it is possible to receive justification without sanctification, to trust in a Savior who does not actually save, to receive a new birth that does not actually give new life, or to have a faith that is not radically repentant despite uniting us to a crucified and risen Christ simply did not compute in their theology. For them Paul had spelled this out with perfect clarity: Those who are Christ's have crucified the flesh with its lusts (Gal. 5:24). To fail to live thus is, as

Calvin vividly pointed out, to "rend [Christ] asunder by . . . muti-
lated faith."[9]

At its darker edges this is the gospel of televangelicalism (doubtless not all equally erroneous theologically) that Tetzel-like peddles
its wares on the small screen, implying, if not actually openly suggesting, that the divine blessing can be purchased financially rather
than received only penitentially.

Almost six hundred years ago, medieval theology at its worst
gave rise to the famous ditty:

> *As soon as the coin in the coffer rings*
> *The soul from purgatory springs.*

But there is a contemporary version found nowhere except in
evangelicalism:

> *As soon as the check in my pocket arrives*
> *An increase in blessing will be your surprise.*

This has become endemic; its influence is pervasive. It is not historic evangelicalism; it is incipient medievalism. Would to God a
Martin Luther might arise within it and cry, "Enough! When our
Lord Jesus Christ said 'repent' he meant that the whole of the Christian life should be one of repentance."

*2. The canon for Christian living has increasingly been sought in a "Spirit-
inspired" living voice within the church rather than in the Spirit's voice heard
in Scripture.*

Again, we need to underline that what we are speaking about
here is a tendency. It is not confined to the charismatic or pentecostal wing of Christendom.

Our concern is not to drag ourselves through the cessationist/non-
cessationist controversy. Whatever our view of that, it is perspicu-
ous that within large sectors of evangelicalism, charismatic and non-
charismatic, continuing "revelation" is welcomed. In a previous
generation this came to clearest expression in those who expected
to find guidance by "listening to the Spirit."

The Reformers and Confessors, including the likes of Calvin and John Owen, were familiar with such "spirituals." Adding to or bypassing the voice of the Spirit in Scripture, they heard his voice directly. Then, as now, some of them claimed to believe in the infallibility of the Scriptures, although they seemed to know little about the doctrine of the sufficiency of Scripture. Sadly, as Calvin seems to have experienced already at the Reformation, it is impossible to discuss the meaning of Scripture with those who claim the direct intervention of the Spirit.

What was once little more than a mystical tendency has become a flood. Is it far from the mark to suggest that those who hold to the Reformers' doctrine of the absolute sufficiency of the voice of the Spirit in Scripture illumined by the work of the Spirit in the heart are a decreasing breed? Both in academic theology as well as at the grassroots level such a position is becoming increasingly regarded as reactionary if not heretical because minority in subscription!

But what has this to do with the medieval church? Just this: The entire medieval church operated on the same principle, even if expressed in a different form. The Spirit speaks outside of Scripture; believers cannot know the detailed guidance of God if they try to depend on their Bible alone. The living voice of the Spirit in the church is essential.

Not only so, but once the "living voice" of the Spirit has been introduced it follows by a kind of psychological inevitability that it is this living voice which becomes the canon for Christian living.

This equation—inscripturated word plus living voice equals divine revelation—lay at the heart of the medieval church's groping in the dark for the power of the gospel. Now, at the end of the second millennium, we are on the verge—and perhaps more than the verge—of being overwhelmed by a parallel phenomenon. The result then was a famine of hearing and understanding the Word of God—all under the guise of what the Spirit was still saying to the church. What of today?

3. *The divine presence was brought to the church by individuals with sacred powers deposited within them and communicated by physical means.*

The invisible church made visible

As the Council of Trent underlined, the medieval doctrine of orders (ordination) imprinted an indelible character on the priest.[10] Through mystical powers the words of the Mass, *hoc est corpus meum,* could change bread and wine into the body and blood of Jesus. While the "accidents" of bread and wine remained, the "substance" became the body and blood of the Lord. With his hands the priest could put Jesus into the believer's mouth.

Today an uncanny parallel is visible wherever cable television can be seen. Admittedly it is no longer Jesus who is given by priestly hands; now it is the Spirit who is bestowed by physical means, apparently at will by the new evangelical priest. Special sanctity is no longer confirmed by the beauty of the fruit of the Spirit, but with signs that are predominantly physical.

The Reformers were not unfamiliar with similar phenomena. In fact, one of the major charges made against them by the Roman Catholic Church was that they did not really have the gospel because they lacked miraculous phenomena.

What we ought to find alarming about contemporary evangelicalism is the extent to which we are impressed by performance rather than piety. In the midst of the plethora of claims to the physical manifestations of the Spirit, will no one raise a voice to cry that it is not physical manifestations, but knowing and being known by Christ in a life of sheer and unquestioned godliness that is the only real evidence of the power of the Spirit?

4. *The worship of God is increasingly presented as a spectator event of visual and sensory power, rather than a verbal event in which we engage in a deep soul dialogue with the Triune God.*

The mood of contemporary evangelicalism is to focus on the centrality of what "happens" in the spectacle of worship rather than on what is heard in worship. Aesthetics, be they artistic or musical, are given priority over holiness. More and more is *seen*, less and less is *heard*. There is a sensory feast, but a hearing famine. Professionalism in worship leadership has become a cheap substitute for genuine access to heaven, however faltering. Drama, not preaching, has become the *didache* of choice.

Performance ——< pretty
"There is a sensory feast, but a hearing famine"

This is a spectrum, of course, not a single point. But most worship is to be found somewhere on that spectrum. Time was when four words brought out goose-bumps on the necks of the congregation—"Let Us Worship God." Not so for twentieth-century evangelicalism. Now there must be color, movement, audiovisual effects. God cannot be known, loved, praised, and trusted for his own sake.

We have lost sight of great things—the fact that Christ himself is the true sanctuary of the new covenant people; that the true beauty is holiness; that when the Lord is in his holy temple all are transfixed with a heart of silence before him.

We have also more subtly lost sight of the transportability of new covenant worship. By comparison with old covenant worship, which depended on the temple, the new was simple *and therefore universalizable.* That was part of the vision that drove on our evangelical forefathers; but much of our worship has become dependent on place, size, and—alas—even technology.

Here, as "confessing evangelicals," we cannot smugly point the finger of scorn and derision at evangelicals who have sold their reformational and confessional heritage for a mess of modern pottage. In how many of our churches is the glory due to the aesthetics rather than to the sheer power of the Spirit and the Word? In how many of our services is there such a sense of God's overwhelming presence in and of itself that outsiders fall on their faces and cry out: "Surely God is in this place!"?

Of course we must offer our very best to God in corporate worship. But "confessing evangelicals" do that by a regulative principle even when they differ on its exact import. They do not think that true worship is a spectator event, where we luxuriate in what others do. It is a *congregational* event, in which Christ mediates our prayers, conducts and leads our praise, and preaches his word to us. He alone is the God-ordained worship leader, the true *leitourgos* of the people of God, the minister in the sanctuary (Heb. 8:2). We dare not obscure this Christ-centered and congregational character of worship, nor make it dependent on anything else than approaching God in the Spirit through Christ with clean hands and a pure heart. Such the Father seeks to worship him!

The tragedy of medieval worship was precisely this: When God was no longer heard with penetrating clarity in the exposition of Scripture—when the sense of the Spirit's presence was no longer a reality—what was given to the people was ritual rather than true liturgy, mystery (Latin!) rather than plain speaking, color rather than clarity of doctrinal understanding, and drama (the medieval plays!) rather than the doctrine that would give them the knowledge of God, nourish their souls, and make them morally and spiritually strong. A spiritual vacuum was created; collapse was inevitable. For years we have been on this slippery slope to neo-medievalism.

In 1978 I had one of the high privileges of my life: speaking at a conference of ministers in Wales with the great Welsh preacher Dr. Martyn Lloyd-Jones. One of his addresses on that occasion was entitled "Extraordinary Phenomena in Revivals of Religion." It was an extraordinary phenomenon in itself: Ninety minutes in length it seemed like fifteen. I was gripped and fascinated to hear of incidents—largely in Wales!—which eyewitnesses had described to him.

Inter alia Dr. Lloyd-Jones mentioned a relatively recent and well-known Welsh evangelist whose "trade mark" was the fact that he himself played an instrument during the evangelistic meetings he conducted. His father on one occasion urged him to lay it aside—his generation of ministers had not needed it. "No, Dad," came the reply, "but *you had the Holy Spirit.*"

Thus we are condemned out of our own mouths.

The tragedy here is that in our worship we are in grave danger of producing a generation of professing Christians who are spiritual infants—feeding them emotionally with what temporarily produces satisfaction but never builds them up.

Dr. James Montgomery Boice well expressed this once in the context of introducing congregational prayer for Sunday school teachers at Tenth Presbyterian Church, Philadelphia. He noted that from the beginning the children are taught small portions of Scripture on which they build until (for example) they are able to recite such chapters of the Bible as Romans 8. Hymns (yes, hymns!) are sung and learned because of their power to teach doctrine (yes, doctrine!).

Why this stark contrast with, if not opposition to, the trends of the time? Here, as I recall, is what Dr. Boice gave as the rationale: "We are living in a time when adults, including Christians, want to behave like children. Here, in our Sunday school, we are training our children to grow up to be Christian adults."

How smug we evangelicals have become—we who know too much about child psychology to care about the Catechism! But, alas, many of today's seminary graduates and ministers know less Christian doctrine than a child in Calvin's Geneva, know less of the misery of sin and the way to the joy of salvation than a boy in Ursinus' Heidelberg, have only half the grasp of man's chief end that a girl in the remote fastnesses of seventeenth-century Scotland might have had, know far less about how to overcome sin than a teenager in John Owen's Oxford.

It should not surprise us, therefore, to discover what novels—and not only novels—evangelicals have been reading of late. Some of those that have been given cult status—("You haven't read_____? My dear, *where have you been?*" we are asked, with a look of blank amazement!)—have expressed a deeply medieval view of the world.

Is the medieval darkness already upon us? Are we equipped to pierce it with the Spirit's sword?

5. *The success of ministry is measured by crowds and cathedrals rather than by the preaching of the cross, by the quality of Christians' lives, and by faithfulness.*

It was the medieval church leaders—bishops and archbishops, cardinals and popes—who built cathedrals, ostensibly *soli Deo gloria*. All this to the neglect of gospel proclamation, the life of the body of Christ as a whole, the needs of the poor, and the evangelism of the world. The "mega-church" is not a modern, but a medieval phenomenon.

Ideal congregational size and specific ecclesiastical architecture thankfully belongs to the *adiaphora*. That is not really the central concern here. Rather it is the almost endemic addiction of contemporary evangelicalism to size and numbers as an index of the success of "my ministry"—a phrase that can itself be strikingly oxymoronic.

Here, too, there is something reminiscent of the Middle Ages. How much indulgence-buying goes on in contemporary church life? How much of the medieval desire for a *kathedra* (throne!) for the leader(s) comes to expression in the staggering buildings we erect "for the glory of God"?

This is not a plea for a new evangelical iconoclasm; smaller is not necessarily more beautiful. But it is to raise the question of reality, depth, and integrity in church life and in Christian ministry. The lust for "bigger" makes us materially and financially vulnerable. But worse, it makes us spiritually vulnerable. For it is hard to say to those on whom we have come to depend materially: "When our Lord Jesus Christ said 'Repent!' he meant that the whole of the Christian life is repentance." And then, what will we make of Thesis 92?

> Away, then, with those prophets who say to Christ's people, "Peace, peace," where there is no peace.

Or, again, what do we make of the spine-chilling Thesis 93?

> Hail, hail to all those prophets who say to Christ's people, "The cross, the cross," where there is no cross.

And can I respond to Thesis 94 with a clear conscience?

> Christians should be exhorted to be zealous to follow Christ, their Head, through penalties, deaths, and hells.

Or Thesis 95?

> And let them thus be more confident of entering heaven through many tribulations rather than through a false assurance of peace.

We may well wish that Luther's Theses had been left in the Latin in which he first penned them and kept within their original arena of academic dispute! But only where these notes ring through our churches can we be sure that we are building Christ's church with gold, silver, and costly stones and not wood, hay, and stubble. And only what we build thus will last in eternity. Everything else will be burned by fire (1 Cor. 3:10–15).

The Grace of Repentance

If repentance is the life-long process of the restoration of sinners, it is, as we have seen, an inescapable, ongoing, and permanent necessity. But how is it to be produced?

Here it is vitally important for us not to write our agenda merely in terms of what is wrong with evangelicalism today. That exercise may be necessary, but it is only partial. It is less than apostolic. For what gives repentance power is not the *guilt* evoked by the Law alone (Rom. 7:7), but the *grace* proclaimed to us in the gospel of our Lord Jesus Christ: it is the kindness of God that leads to repentance (Rom. 2:4); It is because there is forgiveness with God that we live lives of penitential fear (Ps. 130:4). Repentance is a gift of the ascended Christ in his glorious office as Mediator. As the Westminster Divines put it:

> Repentance unto life is an evangelical grace . . . by it, a sinner, out of the sight and sense not only of the danger, but also of the filthiness and odiousness of his sins, as contrary to the holy nature, and righteous law of God; *and upon the apprehension of His mercy in Christ to such as are penitent,* so grieves for and hates his sins, *as to turn from them all unto God, purposing and endeavoring to walk with Him in all the ways of His commandments.*[11]

Wherever we see repentance in the Scriptures, this is the pattern: The revelation of divine holiness in the Law and commandments of God creates the guilt-burden; yet through the weakness of the flesh, Law as command cannot save sinners. But, thank God, what the Law could not do has been accomplished in the incarnation, death, resurrection, and coronation of our Lord Jesus! The kingdom has come; grace enables the guilt-burdened and heart-broken to repent. Repentance is possible only because it is motivated by the promise of grace. Only then do we cry through our tears:

Up is down

> Have mercy . . .
> according to your unfailing love . . .
> according to your great compassion . . .
> Cleanse me . . .
> wash me . . .
> Let me hear joy and gladness . . .
> Hide your face from my sins . . .
> blot out my iniquity . . .
> Create in me a pure heart . . .
> renew a steadfast spirit within me . . .
> Restore to me joy . . .
>
> (Ps. 51:1–12)

The way to the true *theologia gloriae* is by way of the *theologia crucis!* In this God is magnified in the salvation of sinners so that his glory (*kabod*—he is not weightless!) bows us down in humble worship as those whose mouths have been shut and reopened with songs of praise. Then we, too, taste the glory of restored sinners.

But this happens only when we hear the cry, "the cross! the cross!"

Sadly, just here, evangelicalism has become like a latter-day Jonah. It seeks prestige as a power player in the nation, prophesying the only way for the nation's boundaries to be enlarged to fulfill divine destiny (was this the only "prophecy" of Jonah's ministry that anyone could remember? 2 Kings 14:23–25). It seeks to preserve its own *kudos* among its own kind. It sings, but does not find grace really "amazing" or the cross "wondrous"; it wears, but does not bear the cross. The evangelical church offers literature and seminars *largely on what we can accomplish,* rarely on what Christ has accomplished because we cannot. (When did you last read a book or attend a seminar on the cross and on cross-bearing?) It offers having-your-life-together-successfully heedless of the Christ who cannot thus be tamed, house-trained, and thoroughly domesticated, fearful of the chaos God may sovereignly create in order to reorder my life, eschewing the other-worldliness that alone enables us to make a lasting impact on the present world.

But in the purposes of God the way up is the way down. Only as humbled under the mighty hand of God can there be exaltation. We need first to see—Jonah-like—how far down we have sunk; to see our need of grace and the cross; and to find forgiveness and restoration.

As with Jonah, the word of the Lord comes to us with great clarity (cf. Jonah 1:2). We believe in the perspicuity of Scripture:

> Those things which are necessary to be known, believed, and observed, for salvation, are so clearly propounded and opened in some place of Scripture or other, that not only the learned, but the unlearned, in a due use of the ordinary means, may attain unto a sufficient understanding of them.[12]

Our problem does not lie in the parts of Scripture we find difficult to understand! Like Jonah, we turn from the word of the Lord that we *do* understand. We do not read it, we do not love it, we have become almost incapable of meditating upon it; we are careless, if not actually callous about submitting to it.

That we have done so is evidenced, as it was with Jonah, in the way we run from the presence of God (Jonah 1:3, 10). We cannot sit either still or silent before him. Prayer has become the hardest thing in the world for evangelicals to do. Worship together in his presence has been conformed to our convenience mentality.

One of the most obvious evidences of this is the way in which behind all manner of extraordinarily spiritual excuses, the majority of evangelicals leave God in peace even on Sunday after the noon hour strikes! Under the guise of our fear of being black-balled as "sabbatarians" we rob the Lord. As a result we taste less of the cumulative blessing of the worship of the people of God on the Lord's Day. We still honor our evangelical saints, like Robert Murray M'Cheyne, but we find practically incomprehensible their desire to squeeze every last moment out of congregational foretastes of eternal glory.

Have you never, in the dying embers of a Sunday night, rested your head on the pillow with wet eyes because the day of congregating in the presence of God does not yet last forever? Are we in danger of so being squeezed into this world's mold that Christ has this against us: We have lost our first love? Or do we still believe *here and now* that in his presence is fullness of joy and at his right hand pleasures for evermore?

Poor Jonah: He ran away from the presence of the Lord. Where was the blessedness he knew when first he saw the Lord? But then, what about my "soul-refreshing view" of the presence of Jehovah-Jesus and his Word (Cowper)?

Recovery

Is there a way back? Do we still have a future? Yes, there is a way back. There is the sign of Jonah: the cross. And God has his ways of preparing winds to pursue us, great fish to swallow us, dark bellies which—as Calvin says—become hospitals to heal us of our deathly sickness. But we may well need "distress" as a community to make us call on the Lord (Jonah 2:2) and turn back to his presence and his word.

It is an amazing, if revealing, *faux-pas* when liberal Old Testament scholars have suggested that the prayer of Jonah 2 is simply a smart piece of authorial creativity because it is virtually a catena of quotations from the Psalms. (Have they never attended a church prayer meeting?) But that is precisely the point. The man could not get enough of Scripture. Like all who deeply repent he devoured them, turned them into prayer, wanted to bathe in and feed upon them, and longed to put into practice everything they commanded. What he had vowed he would make good (Jonah 2:9).

And, inevitably, he sought the presence of God and the worship of God. Banished in exile, he wanted his captivity to end. He wanted to be in the temple (Jonah 2:4, 7)—where the portrayal of forgiveness could be found, where the praise of God could be heard, where the people of God could be met, where encouragement to keep his vows could be found.

When Jonah thus repented, it was inevitable that his heart would be moved with compassion for the lost who "cling to worthless idols [and] forfeit the grace that could be theirs" (Jonah 2:8). But that happened only when he realized the grip the idols of his own heart had on him, and how tightly he had gripped them. Only then did it dawn on him with fresh power that "Salvation comes from the

LORD" (2:9). When that happens to us, true evangelical repentance becomes the sweetest pain in the whole world.

Would we had a baptism of it!

Clearly this has the most general application. But if we are cut to the heart by the need for repentance, what are *we* to do that there may be salvation?

By God's grace we need, first of all, to be better men and women. We need to be godly, not merely efficient. We need to resolve that we will never defile ourselves in the City of this World with Babylonian meat and believe that the bread and water of the City of God will make us spiritually fat and healthy and fill us with the wisdom of heaven. We need to be more heavenly-minded, more Christ-centered, more ready to bear the cross; we need to be more sin-mortifying and Christ-imaging men and women. It is as simple as that. But how?

Evangelicalism is a noble tradition. Shall we not learn from our forefathers? They determined to live in the presence of God; they gathered to seek his presence and to listen to his voice in the exposition and application of Scripture; they built communities of Christ with precious stones hewn at great cost from deep quarries; they eschewed wood and hay and stubble. They knew they would stand before the judgment seat of Christ to receive what was due them for the things they had done in the body—and so they lived and labored, prayed and built for eternity. And so must we.

They prayed, and asked for divine blessing. And they were heard. Alas, we have not, because we ask not; and even when we ask, it is too often to fulfill our own ungodly lusts (cf. James 4:2–3).

What must we do? We must feel the weight of the truth that the kingdom has come in Jesus Christ; we must repent and believe the gospel.

Confession

This chapter focuses on *Repentance, Recovery, and Confession*. Thus, we come, in conclusion, to *confession*—to homologating the judgment of Almighty God upon our lives and ministries.

Unlike our forefathers, we do this with great infrequency, for evangelicalism has tended to individualize and privatize. Moreover, who of us is capable of bearing the weight of being the mouthpiece of the confession of such sins as ours? We all need to *be led* in confessing sin and failure, for we are neophytes in this matter. But perhaps again our forefathers can come to our aid.

The Confession and Catechism drawn up by the Westminster Assembly between 1643 and 1648 are well known. Less well known is the fact that four years later the ministers of the Church of Scotland, having embraced these grand doctrinal statements, recognized their need not only to confess the doctrines of the faith but also the sins of their lives as an essential beginning point for ongoing repentance.

Those were critical, but by no means wholly barren days spiritually, any more than our own days are wholly barren. There were many evidences of God's preserving goodness; there were numerous ministries of outstanding godliness, grace, power, and fruitfulness. Those were days when Puritan giants could be met in the streets of London, Oxford, and many other places. Indeed, in 1650 an English merchant returning from a visit to Scotland was able to say:

> Great and good news! I went to St. Andrews, where I heard a sweet majestic-looking man [Robert Blair], and he showed me *the majesty of God*. After him I heard a little fair man [Samuel Rutherford] and he showed me *the loveliness of Christ*. I then went to Irvine, where I heard a well-favored proper old man with a long beard [David Dickson] and that man showed me *all my heart*.[13]

Yet it is surely evidence of the stirrings of God that such Christian leaders corporately confess their faults. And we may learn from their example what it is that the Lord requires of us. What follows is part of their confession of their sins *as Christian leaders*. It is applicable to all Christians. For as the Westminster Confession notes, true evangelical repentance calls each of us "to repent of his particular sins particularly."[14]

> Ignorance of God, want [lack] of nearness with him, and taking up little of God in reading, meditating and speaking of him;

exceeding great selfishness in all that we do; acting from ourselves, for ourselves, and to ourselves.

Not caring how faithful and negligent others were, so being it might contribute a testimony to our faithfulness and diligence, but being rather content, if not rejoicing, at their faults.

Least delight in those things wherein lieth our nearest communion with God; great inconstancy in our walk with God, and neglect of acknowledging him in all our ways. In going about duties, least careful about those things which are most remote from the eyes of men. Seldom in secret prayer with God, except to fit for public performance; and even that much neglected, or gone about very superficially.

Glad to find excuses for the neglect of our duties. Neglecting the reading of Scripture in secret, for edifying ourselves as Christians. . . . Not given to reflect upon our own ways, nor allowing conviction to have a thorough work upon us; deceiving ourselves by resting upon absence from and abhorrence of evils from the light of a natural conscience, and looking upon the same as an evidence of a real change of state and nature. Evil guarding of and watching over the heart, and carelessness in self-searching; which makes much unacquaintedness with ourselves and estrangedness from God.

Not esteeming the cross of Christ and sufferings for his name, honourable, but rather shifting sufferings from self-love.

Not laying to heart the sad and heavy sufferings of the people of God abroad, and the not-thriving of the kingdom of Jesus Christ and the power of godliness among them.

Refined hypocrisy; desiring to appear what, indeed, we are not. Studying more to learn the language of God's people than their exercise. Artificial confessing of sin, without repentance; professing to declare iniquity, and not resolving to be sorry for sin. Confession in secret much slighted, even of those things whereof we are convicted.

Readier to search out and censure faults in others than to see or deal with them in ourselves. Accounting of our estate and way according to the estimate that others have of us.

Estimation of men, as they agree or disagree from us.

Fruitless conversing ordinarily with others, for the worse rather than for the better. Foolish jesting away of time with . . . useless discourse.

Slighting of fellowship with those by whom we might profit. Desiring more to converse with those that might better us by their talents than with such as might edify us by their graces.

Not studying opportunities of doing good to others. Shifting of prayer and other duties when called thereto . . . loving our pleasures more than God. Taking little or no time to Christian discourse with young men trained up for the ministry. . . .

Not praying for men of a contrary judgment, but using reservedness and distance from them; being more ready to speak *of* them than to them, or to God *for* them. Not weighed with the failings and miscarriages of others, but rather taking advantage thereof for justifying ourselves. Talking of and sporting at the faults of others, rather than compassionating of them.

Carelessness in employing Christ, and drawing virtues out of him, for enabling us to preach in the Spirit and in power. In praying for assistance we pray more for assistance to the messenger than to the message which we carry, not caring what becomes of the Word, if we be with some measure of assistance carried on in the duty.

Exceeding great neglect and unskillfulness to set forth the excellencies and usefulness of (and the necessity of an interest in) Jesus Christ. . . . Speaking of Christ more by hearsay than from knowledge and experience, or any real impression of him upon the heart. . . . Want of sobriety in preaching the gospel; not savouring anything but what is new; so that the substantials of religion bear but little bulk.

Not preaching Christ in the simplicity of the gospel, nor ourselves the people's servants, for Christ's sake. Preaching of Christ, not that the people may know him, but that they may think we know much of him. . . . Not preaching with bowels of compassion to them that are in hazard [danger] to perish.

Bitterness, instead of zeal, in speaking against malignants, sectarians and other scandalous persons. . . . Too much eyeing our own credit and applause; and being pleased with it when we get it, and unsatisfied when it is wanting. . . . Not making all the counsel of God known to his people.[15]

There is more; and there is surely much more we need to confess. Ought we not to make a beginning now? For in the broadest sense it remains true: Unless we repent, we will all—evangelicals, confessing evangelicals, Reformed, Lutheran, Baptist, and Congregationalist alike—likewise perish.

From depths of woe I raise to thee
The voice of lamentation;
Lord, turn a gracious ear to me
And hear my supplication:
If thou iniquities dost mark,
Our secret sins and misdeeds dark,
O who shall stand before thee?

To wash away the crimson stain,
Grace, grace alone availeth;
Our works, alas! are all in vain;
In much the best life faileth:
No man can glory in thy sight,
All must alike confess thy might,
And live alone by mercy.

Therefore my trust is in the Lord,
And not in mine own merit;
On him my soul shall rest, his Word
Upholds my fainting spirit:
His promised mercy is my fort;
My comfort and my sweet support;
I wait for it with patience.

What though I wait the live-long night,
And till the dawn appeareth,
My heart still trusteth in his might;
It doubteth not nor feareth:

Do thus, O ye of Israel's seed,
Ye of the Spirit born indeed;
And wait till God appeareth.

Though great our sins and sore our woes
His grace much more aboundeth;
His helping love no limit knows,
Our utmost need it soundeth.
Our Shepherd good and true is he,
Who will at last his Israel free
From all their sin and sorrow.

(Based on Martin Luther's rendering of Psalm 130)

We are calling the church,

amidst our dying culture,

to repent of its worldliness,

to recover and confess the truth of God's

Word

as did the Reformers,

and **to see that truth embodied**

in doctrine, worship, and life.

7

The Reformation of Worship

W. Robert Godfrey

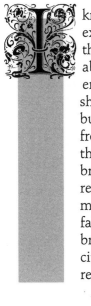

know that Messiah is coming. When he comes, he will explain everything to us" (John 4:25). With these words the Samaritan woman began to reflect on her remarkable meeting with Jesus. He had spoken to her of several matters: living water, her husband, and proper worship. At first glance his conversation seems disjointed, but his words led her to faith and ultimately led many from her village to faith as well. He taught her about the water of eternal life that he as God's Messiah brought into the world. He challenged her immoral life, reminding her that God's will is for a chaste and godly marriage. He called her away from worship that was false to new covenant worship in spirit and truth. In his brief but comprehensive words Jesus explained true discipleship, showing that his disciples accept the truth, repent of their sins, and faithfully worship God.

For Christians who have understood the teaching of Jesus, doctrine, worship, and life have always been intimately intertwined and interconnected. Faith involves the truth of God (doctrine), meeting with God (worship), and serving God (life). The inseparability of these three elements can often be seen in the Scriptures and in the history of God's people.

For example, when Paul wrote to the Colossians, he connected these themes. He discussed the doctrines of the divinity of Christ and his saving work on the cross (Col. 2:9–15). He refuted a variety of errors about worship, concluding with a warning against all forms of "self-imposed worship" (2:16–23). He called the Colossians to holiness by putting to death their fallen nature and by living in and for Christ (3:1–14). Paul expressed the interdependence of these three in just two verses, 3:4–5: "When Christ, who is your life, appears, then you also will appear with him in glory. Put to death, therefore, whatever belongs to your earthly nature: sexual immorality, impurity, lust, evil desires and greed, which is idolatry." The *doctrine* of the glorious return of Christ should lead the Christian to a *life* of mortifying the flesh, recognizing that vices such as greed are idolatry, a form of false *worship*.

Worship through the Centuries

Throughout the centuries Christians have seen this same connection of doctrine, worship, and life. Augustine, for example, expressed it clearly in his *Confessions* as he discussed his conversion. His conversion had an intellectual dimension as he accepted the truth of Christian doctrine. It had a moral dimension as he abandoned his carnal habits and embraced chastity. It had a sacramental dimension as he was baptized and became a full part of Christ's worshiping community.[1]

The Reformers insisted on the need for reform in all three areas. Martin Luther related doctrine, worship, and life as essential to the Reformation in his attack on the Mass. He wrote in the Smalcald Articles: "The Mass in the papacy must be regarded as the greatest and most horrible abomination because it runs into direct and violent conflict with this fundamental article [of Christ and faith]. Yet, above and beyond all others, it has been the supreme and most precious of the papal idolatries. . . . Since such countless and unspeakable abuses have arisen everywhere through the buying and selling of Masses, it would be prudent to do without the Mass for no other reason than to curb such abuses."[2] Luther taught that Christians must reject the Roman Mass because it attacks sound doctrine, is false worship, and leads to corruption of life.

Luther made a similar point in a moment of reflection upon his life and experiences recorded in his *Table Talk.* He said, "I chose twenty-one saints and prayed to three every day when I celebrated mass; thus I completed the number every week. I prayed especially to the Blessed Virgin, who with her womanly heart would compassionately appease her Son. Ah, if the article on justification hadn't fallen, the brotherhoods, pilgrimages, masses, invocation of saints, etc., would have found no place in the church. If it falls again (which may God prevent!) these idols will return."[3] Again doctrine, worship, and life are intimately interrelated.

Similarly John Calvin connected these three as he thought about the heart of the Reformation: "There are three things on which the safety of the Church is founded, viz., doctrine, discipline, and the sacraments, and to these a fourth is added, viz., ceremonies, by which to exercise the people in offices of piety."[4] In another place Calvin imagined a Christian at prayer who laments that the medieval church has offered teachings "which could neither properly train me to the legitimate worship of thy Deity, nor pave the way for me to a sure hope of salvation, nor train me aright for the duties of the Christian life."[5] He makes the same point again as he reflects on the beginning of the Reformation: "When God raised up Luther and others, who held forth a torch to light us into the way of salvation, and who, by their ministry, founded and reared our churches, those heads of doctrine in which the truth of our religion, those in which the salvation of men are comprehended, were in a measure obsolete. We maintain that the use of the sacraments was in many ways vitiated and polluted. And we maintain that the government of the Church was converted into a species of foul and insufferable tyranny."[6] The doctrine of salvation, worship with pure sacraments, and life in the church were basic for Calvin to the reform of Christianity.

This Reformation concern continued among orthodox Protestants. For example, the Puritans in the seventeenth century produced a great summary of doctrine in the Westminster Confession of Faith. But that assembly also prepared both a Psalter for singing God's praise and a directory to guide public worship. The Westminster Assembly further showed its concern for faithful Christian living in the detailed exposition of the Ten Commandments that it made part of its Larger Catechism.

Although the three elements of doctrine, worship, and life always remain affected by one another, at times in modern church history one element has seemed more prominent than the others. Doctrine was preeminent in the controversy between liberalism and fundamentalism in the 1920s and 1930s. Worship was the center of Scottish Presbyterian struggles in the seventeenth century. Life has dominated a variety of modern movements that primarily reacted against the perception of formalism and deadness in the church. Pietism, Methodism, revivalism, the holiness movement, and Pentecostalism all stress the call to life.

In the past thirty years the evangelical movement has expressed concerns in all three of these areas. Evangelicals have worked to preserve sound doctrine in their defense of the inerrancy of the Scriptures. They have manifested their moral commitment in their opposition to abortion. They have also undertaken extensive experimentation in the public worship of God.

Changes in Worship

Recent evangelical experiments in worship are particularly significant for two reasons. First, they represent the most widespread changes in Protestant public worship since the Reformation. While various changes in worship had occurred earlier, they came much more slowly and were much less radical. Second, the contemporary changes in worship offer perhaps the best perspective from which to evaluate the health of evangelicalism today. We can effectively discern the spiritual vitality and biblical fidelity of contemporary evangelicalism by looking at the changing character of its worship.

Variety has long characterized evangelicals in their practice of worship, from the high Anglican liturgy to the wildly charismatic. But beyond these historic differences evangelicals from many traditions in recent years have introduced some common, specific changes in worship in at least five areas. First, many have added new elements to worship. Second, many have changed the character of traditional elements of the service. Third, many have altered the quantity, character, and role of music in the service. Fourth, churches have shown a willingness to involve many more people in leading worship. Fifth, many churches have made changes in the times of their worship.

These changes invite more detailed scrutiny.

Many congregations have added a variety of new elements to their worship. Some have added liturgical dance and dramatic or humorous skits. Some have used visual aids—from banners to slides and films. Some have added a variety of Pentecostal activities, from being slain in the Spirit to holy laughter. Some have added popcorn and Super Bowl viewing—although perhaps not as an act of worship proper.

Many congregations have changed the character of traditional elements of worship. Worship leaders read much shorter passages of the Bible and spend much less time in prayer. Sermons are more likely to be psychological rather than theological or expository. How to manage stress or time or money seem to be among the most pressing spiritual issues of our time. The Lord's Supper is apt to be either eliminated or elaborated with new ceremony and symbolism.

Many churches have seen major changes in the area of music. They give much more time to music and make use of a greater variety of instruments and of more special music, especially soloists and choirs. The style of music has also changed in many churches. Classical music and traditional hymnody have given way to praise songs in styles ranging from Christian rock or pop to country and western. Even more important, the role of music has changed for many. Whereas traditionally music was an important part of the dialogue between God and his people, for many it has become the heart of worship, even called the "Praise and Worship" part of the service. Music seems to have become for some a new sacrament, mediating the presence and experience of God, establishing a mystical bond between God and the worshiper. With eyes closed and hands in the air worshipers repeat simple phrases that become Christian mantras.

Many churches have abandoned the historic practice of having an ordained minister lead the service. Various parts of the service are now led by professionals or members of the congregation. In some places no part of the service—even sermon, sacrament, or benediction—seems reserved for the minister.

A number of churches have made changes in the time of worship. The Sunday evening service has died in many places. The Saturday evening service has emerged as a new time of worship for the busy, who save Sunday for work or recreation. Some churches give much more attention to the holy days of the church year. Christmas receives at least a month of preparation in many churches (as well as in the stores). But, strangely, services are often not held on Christmas Day itself.

In spite of the magnitude of these changes, an amazingly small amount of discussion or controversy has attended their introduction. To be sure some local congregations have had troubles and some articles and books have appeared on worship. But relative to the impact of the changes on the life of the church, the discussion about them has been remarkably mild. The ease with which such momentous changes have taken place points to the dissatisfaction prevalent among evangelicals with traditional worship and gives an insight into the contemporary evangelical mind.

Change without Reflection

Why have these changes occurred so easily and in many cases with so little reflection? Many evangelicals had concluded that their public worship was marginal, ineffective, dull, and irrelevant. More specifically, first, for a long time many evangelicals have not seen public worship as being at the heart of their Christian life and experience. Indeed a distinctive role for public worship diminished as many stressed that all of life was worship and that worship could take many other forms than just the worship of the whole congregation together. For many the real focus of their Christian lives became small groups for Bible study, prayer, fellowship, and discipleship. Small groups seem to offer more personal and heart-felt prayer, more intimate and meaningful fellowship, more relevant and effective teaching. For others the center became para-ecclesiastical organizations of service, education, and evangelism. Probably few evangelicals today would agree with Calvin that listening to a sermon is more important spiritually then reading the Bible privately.

Second, leaders have introduced many changes to public worship in the name of evangelism. A passion for evangelism has long been a central concern of evangelicals. So an argument that new elements of worship (whether drama or dancing or drums—or even an entire service designed for "seekers") will enhance evangelism and church growth becomes irresistible. So whether real evangelism will occur or not, the changes are made.

Third, the changes have made worship much more interesting and engaging for many. In a culture where the images of television and the cinema are powerful and nearly omnipresent, new uses of the visual are very appealing. In a culture where the music from radio, CD, and tape is varied and professional, American evangelicals are accustomed to being entertained. The traditional church—with many words, slow pace, and antique music—appears tedious and boring. The changes seem to put vitality back into worship.

Fourth, these changes represent an acceleration and extension of changes that have been taking place in evangelical worship for around two hundred years. Particularly the rise of revivalism as the dominant form of evangelicalism in nineteenth-century America established tendencies in worship that have culminated in what we see today.[7] The altar call became a new element in many worship services. Sermons often became primarily evangelistic in character. Suspicion of the professional clergy and education encouraged the rise of lay preachers, of whom Dwight L. Moody was the most notable. In music the Psalms were first replaced by the hymns of Watts and Wesley and they in turn gave way to revival songs that seemed to decline steadily in the quality of their theological content, poetry, and music. Cantatas and music programs replaced worship services at times. Choirs, special music, and revival hymns became important for setting the mood of worship. The 1914 authorized biography of Billy Sunday reported of his meetings: "From half an hour to an hour of this varied music introduces each service. When the evangelist himself is ready to preach, the crowd has been worked up into a glow and fervor that make it receptive to his message."[8]

Fifth, evangelicals have not considered how many contemporary changes in worship they have borrowed from Pentecostal or charismatic churches: the spontaneous style, the multiple leadership, the expression of individual thoughts and feelings, the character of the music, and the dramatic. (Of course the charismatic worship is itself an extension of some elements of the earlier revivalism.) Many of these changes rest on charismatic theologies of spirituality, worship, and ministry. Do evangelicals really want to embrace these theologies and all that such theologies entail?

Sixth, the ready acceptance of these changes shows how much evangelicals have accommodated themselves to modern culture. These changes all seem natural in a culture that tends to be democratized, individualistic, anti-intellectual, pragmatic, and optimistic. In a democratized and individualistic culture it seems fully appropriate that each member of the congregation should be able to lead in worship and that each should find forms of worship and music that are attractive and fulfilling. In an anti-intellectual and pragmatic culture forms of worship will seem proper that appeal more to the emotions than the mind, that are immediately accessible and draw crowds rather than are challenging or disciplined. Entertainment replaces edification. As D. G. Hart has aptly put it in an article entitled "Post-Modern Evangelical Worship": "Indeed, contemporary worship—and church life for that matter—depends increasingly on the products of pop culture. . . . Rather than growing up and adopting the broader range of experiences that characterizes adulthood, evangelicals . . . want to recover and perpetuate the experiences of adolescence."[9] In an optimistic culture churches will assume that many are seeking God and that the message of sin, judgment, and hell must be muted.

Reflection on Change

This new situation calls for careful consideration. It requires reflection not only on the new trends in worship, but also on the character of contemporary evangelicalism. How should we evaluate the new worship and the new evangelicals?

Obviously many see these changes in a positive light. Robert Webber, for example, in his work *Signs of Wonder,*[10] has written very positively of the ways in which liturgical, charismatic, and traditional Protestant churches have been borrowing from each other in worship. He sees this as evidence of renewal in all these groups.

Such positive evaluation seems profoundly wrong, however, from a variety of perspectives. In keeping with modern culture we might evaluate the changes pragmatically. Have the churches grown? Have the churches successfully evangelized many? Have Christians achieved new levels of faith, devotion, love, and service? Anecdotally one might conclude that many churches have succeeded. Stories abound among evangelicals about churches growing and churches planted by the use of the new measures of the new worship. But do these reports give a true picture of contemporary church experience?

Sadly these stories more often seem to reflect the evangelical addiction to superlatives rather than accurate reporting. Most everything we do is heralded as the best ever. Not long ago a full-page advertisement in a major newspaper for an evangelistic meeting promised the greatest manifestation of the power of God in the history of the world. Evangelicals seem always "at unique moments of opportunity" to be met "with the greatest resources ever available."

Evangelical superlatives are one manifestation of the legacy of Charles Finney, who saw excitement as the key to evangelical success. He wrote: "God has found it necessary to take advantage of the excitability there is in mankind, to produce powerful excitements among them, before He can lead them to obey."[11] "There must be excitement sufficient to wake up the dormant moral powers, and roll back the tide of degradation and sin."[12] To stimulate that excitement Finney developed his "new measures"—what J. I. Packer somewhere called "religious technology." Finney declared, "The object of our measures is to gain attention and you *must* have something new."[13]

The problem is that once one gets beyond anecdotes about the new, exciting achievements, the evidence for evangelical success is sadly wanting. America is not experiencing a revival of faith or holiness. Christians may be moving from one congregation to another, but Christianity does not seem to be growing overall.[14] Indeed evangelicalism seems weaker and less influential for the gospel than ever. It has failed according to its own criteria of success.[15]

The most important evaluation of evangelicalism and its worship, however, needs to be biblical and theological. The only criteria for faithfulness that matter are God's, and those criteria can only be found in the Scriptures.

A Theology of Worship

The Scriptures use the word "worship" in a variety of ways. Worship may refer to the whole of life (Rom. 12:1–2). It may also refer to various forms of personal or informal devotion (for example, Deut. 6:4–9). Of particular interest to us is worship as the official gathering of the covenant people to meet with God (for example, Acts 2:42; Heb. 10:25).

Corporate worship is meeting with God. Psalm 74:8 speaks of the places of Israel's worship as "meeting places with God." Even before the fall in the Garden of Eden man needed concentrated time with God. As finite beings humans need specific times and opportunities to focus on God. Israel worshiped around a tabernacle that was known as the Tent of Meeting. When the temple was built, Israel gathered at that dwelling of God to meet with him. In the new covenant the gathering of the Christian community is a meeting of God in the heavenly temple—a theme developed, for example, in Hebrews 10 and 12.

This meeting with God anticipates the everlasting fellowship that God will have with his people in a new heaven and a new earth. The whole purpose of salvation is that the broken relationship between God and man might be overcome so that true fellowship might be restored. The importance of worship is remarkably expressed in this statement of Calvin: "To debate about the mode in which men obtain salvation, and say nothing of the mode in which God may be duly worshipped, is too absurd."[16]

God has always taken his worship very seriously. He speaks of his worship not only in the Second Commandment, but at least implicitly in the first four of the Ten Commandments. He offers serious warnings about worship throughout the Law (for example, Deut. 4). He visits terrible judgment on those who pervert his worship (for example, Lev. 10 and 2 Chron. 26). The same concern is clear in the New Testament. Worship is a concern of Jesus and Paul. Hebrews 12:28–29 sums up this concern well: "Let us be thankful, and so worship God acceptably with reverence and awe, for our 'God is a consuming fire.'"

An Evaluation of Worship

God's concern about his worship must lead evangelicals to much more careful evaluation of their practice of worship. First, evangelicals must reconsider the new elements introduced into worship. Are visual elements such as drama, dance, and film acceptable to God? They do not seem consistent with a thoughtful application of the Second Commandment. Rather, they seem more like strange fire offered to the Lord (Lev. 10:1). God in Scripture never approved of creativity or innovation in worship. How can evangelicals so blithely assume God approves of their new activities?

These elements need to be rigorously subjected to the Scriptures. Evangelical failure to do so shows that the Bible does not function in a central way in the life and thought of many. Too many evangelicals are content to take themes or motifs from Scripture, but not to study carefully its details or see it as presenting a coherent, systematic truth. Evangelicals need to see that worship must be Word-directed in specifics, not just in a general, vague way.

For many evangelicals the justification of their new worship is rooted in their sincerity. Worship must certainly be sincere to be acceptable to God. But sincerity by itself does not make worship acceptable to God. The worshipers of Baal in Elijah's day were sincere. Many worshipers of Yahweh in Samaria were sincere. But God rejected such worship as violations of the First or Second Commandment. Sincerity does not justify false worship any more than it does false doctrine or disobedient living.

Worship that is simple and spiritual will encourage Christian living that is disciplined and consistent. It will lead evangelicals back to the Bible. Such worship will truly build up the body of Christ in doctrine and in life.

Second, evangelicals must reexamine the ways in which they have changed the traditional elements of worship. Sermons must again be closely expository so that the church really hears God's Word, not human opinions. The exposition of the Word in its richness will confront our sinful ideas, values, and ways, insuring that worship will not be simply soothing and comforting. The Bible must be read as a central act of worship—not only to inform but as an act of reverence and thanks to a God who has revealed himself. Prayer must be restored as the congregation's privilege to speak to the God who draws near to them. The sacraments must be seen as the kindness of the Lord in giving a visible expression to the gospel.

The historic elements of worship reflected a sense of the greatness and presence of God. Evangelicals must recapture a profoundly God-centered worship and move away from their increasingly man-centered worship. As Calvin wrote: "It is not very sound theology to confine a man's thoughts so much to himself, and not to set before him, as the prime motive of his existence, zeal to illustrate the glory of God. For we are born first of all for God, and not for ourselves."[17]

The Christian life will flourish in a context where a vital relationship with God according to his Word is cultivated. Meeting with God in truth will strengthen Christian living.

Third, evangelicals must look carefully at their music. Music is a key way to express emotion in worship. But contemporary worship too often is only concerned with the emotion of joy—and that in a very superficial way. The Bible certainly stresses joy, but it equally stresses reverence. Psalm 2:11 says, "Serve the LORD with fear and rejoice with trembling." Reverence and joy must both be expressed in worship.

Joy and reverence reflect the character of God, who is just and merciful, holy and loving. Worship that is only joyful serves a God stripped of half his attributes. It produces a gospel that tells of peace where there is no peace. It severs Law from gospel and repentance from faith.

The worship songs of the church must follow the pattern of the Psalter that praises the character and great works of God. Such praise is not composed of the repetition of phrases or bad poetry. It is verbally rich, emotionally varied, and full of content.

Such praise will fill the minds and hearts of God's people with the truth of God and with love for God as he truly is. It will fill minds with truth for meditation. It will encourage the people of God to holy living.

Fourth, many evangelicals have diminished the role of the minister in leading worship and multiplied the number of worship leaders. Such actions are in accord with a democratic culture and are often justified by an appeal to the doctrine of the priesthood of all believers. But the change has often brought to leadership people who are not educated or experienced for that role. More important, such people have not been called or set aside by the congregation for that work.

Evangelicals need to regain a theology of office and ministry. One of Christ's great gifts to his church, according to Ephesians 4, is the office of pastors and teachers. Those gifted and called by Christ and his church need to lead the people of God in their worship carefully in accordance with the Word.

Such leadership will help Christians in all their living reflect on the importance of the structures and authorities that God has appointed. The decline of respect for authorities, whether parents, teachers, employers, or government authorities, is a major problem of our time. The church must be an example to society in its respect for the ministers and elders that Christ has established in his church.

Fifth, evangelicals have changed the time of worship to make worship easier and more accessible. But have the evangelicals understood the call of the Lord to sanctify the Lord's Day? There is a Lord's Day in the new covenant—Revelation 1:10—and by sanctifying it the people of God learn obedience and self-denial. Real Christianity is not easy, but embraces the discipline and blessing of rest and worship on the Lord's Day. True faith delights to spend time with God. It treasures time for devotion, learning, and service. It does not seek to get worship over with, but seeks to follow the revealed pattern of a day with God.

Evangelicals in relation to worship, doctrine, and life have tended to become minimalists. Too many are asking, What is the least I can do and what is the easiest way to do it to be a disciple of Jesus Christ? Evangelicals must remember—of all things—the Great Commission (Matt. 28:18–20). There Jesus declared what true discipleship is. It has a doctrinal dimension: Disciples must acknowledge Jesus as possessing all authority in heaven and on earth. It has a worship dimension: Disciples must be baptized in the name of the Father and the Son and the Holy Spirit. It has a life dimension: Disciples are to obey everything God has commanded. Evangelicals must recapture the fullness of biblical religion.

Repentance and Reformation

This brief analysis and evaluation of evangelicals and contemporary worship will not commend itself to everyone. Some will reject it entirely. Others will object to one or more points in it. But it will serve its most important function if it provokes a spirited discussion of these issues. In our day evangelicals need to engage in more debate on matters of doctrine, worship, and life.

True ecumenicity will require a return to polemical theology which, while scrupulously civil and honest, is also sharp and spirited. Polemic cannot only be a treasured part of Christianity's heroic past, but needs to be part of our present. Defenders of the faith today must follow in the train of Athanasius and Augustine, of Luther and Calvin, of J. Gresham Machen and Robert Preus. We must not be emasculated by what James Hunter has rightly called our "ethic of civility," where we strive always not only to tolerate, but to be tolerable.[18] As Calvin wrote: "For then only do pastors edify the Church, when, besides leading docile souls to Christ placidly, as with the hand, they are also armed to repel the machinations of those who strive to impede the work of God."[19]

In a spirited defense of the Reformation Calvin attacked the papacy, daring anyone "to give the name of Christ's Vicar to one who, after routing the truth of Christ, extinguishing the light of the gospel, overthrowing the salvation of men, corrupting and profaning the worship of God, and trampling down and tearing to pieces all his sacred institutions, domineers like a barbarian."[20] In our culture of civility such polemic will strike many as excessive. But for Calvin the gospel was at stake. He followed the example of the Apostle Paul in his writing to the Galatians. What language should we use in an evangelical world where some teach doctrines of God and salvation worse than any pope; where some promote worship that is more self-indulgent and self-righteous than any pope; where some ignore the Law of God more flagrantly than any pope? So-called evangelicals promote anti-Christian doctrine teaching the mutability of God and denying the forensic character of justification.[21] They debase worship with unholy laughter, false prophecy, and vain repetition. They corrupt Christian living by condoning divorce, homosexuality, abortion, and infanticide.[22]

B. B. Warfield once observed of the theology of Charles Finney: "God might be eliminated from it entirely without essentially changing its character."[23] The same might be said of too much of contemporary evangelicalism. We need sharper analysis and pointed refutation. We need to ask whether Calvin's judgment of the medieval church applies also to us: "They have contaminated the pure worship of God by impious superstitions, and involved the doctrine both of faith and repentance in endless errors; that by darkness of various sorts they have not only obscured but almost extinguished the virtue and grace of Christ; and by unworthy methods have adulterated the Sacrament."[24]

Today as always doctrine, worship, and life remain closely interdependent. Where doctrine teaches that man is good and God is benevolent, worship will be upbeat—the children's playroom—and life will be oriented to self-fulfillment. Where worship focuses on human needs and entertainment, the doctrine of God, sin, and grace will wither and life will become self-centered. Where life is self-indulgent, doctrine and worship will also be self-indulgent.

Today evangelicals need careful self-examination as we consider their doctrine, worship, and life. We need to meditate on passages of Scripture such as Deuteronomy 4.

> Hear now, O Israel, the decrees and laws I am about to teach you. Follow them so that you may live and may go in and take possession of the land that the LORD, the God of your fathers is giving you. Do not add to what I command you and do not subtract from it, but keep the commands of the LORD your God that I give you.... Observe them carefully, for this will show your wisdom and understanding to the nations, who will hear about all these decrees and say, "Surely this great nation is a wise and understanding people." What other nation is so great as to have their gods near them the way the LORD our God is near us whenever we pray to him? ... Be careful not to forget the covenant of the LORD your God that he made with you; do not make for yourselves an idol in the form of anything the LORD your God has forbidden. For the LORD your God is a consuming fire, a jealous God (Deut. 4:1, 2, 6, 7, 23, 24).

Evangelicals need to repent. Too often we have replaced the consuming fire with a mild-mannered God; replaced the worship of the invisible God with some forms of human invention; replaced the moral law of God with the fulfillment of felt-needs. J. B. Phillips decades ago stimulated evangelicals with his book, *Your God Is Too Small.* Today we need a book entitled, *Your God Is Too Bland* or even, perhaps, *Your God Is a Pagan Idol.* Evangelicals need a spirit of repentance that will lead to a thorough reformation of doctrine, worship, and life.

8

Reformation in Doctrine, Worship, and Life

James Montgomery Boice

his is a practical chapter, which suggests what items need to be recovered in the doctrine, worship, and life of our churches if God's people are to become an effective presence for good in American society today. It assumes the points argued in the earlier chapters: (1) that the evangelical church has become secular in the abandonment of its theological heritage for pragmatism, and (2) that the truths that need to be recovered are those of the Protestant Reformers who honored God as the author and perfecter of the church's faith. These truths are expressed in part by the *"sola's"*: *sola Scriptura, sola fide, solus Christus, sola gratia,* and *soli Deo gloria.*

In this chapter I explore what a serious recovery of those and other important Reformation doctrines might involve as our churches go about their business:

173

governing what they teach, guiding the manner in which they encourage and conduct worship, and forming the kind of communal life they need to model before the watching world.

Reformation in Doctrine

We live in an age of weak and in places nearly nonexistent theology, especially among evangelicals who are supposed to understand and affirm it. So to speak about a recovery of doctrine is, on one level at least, to speak about the broadest possible recovery. It is to recover all the major doctrines of all the creeds. We need to teach about God and his attributes, the nature of man as God made him and as fallen, the work of Jesus Christ in accomplishing our salvation (recovering the great biblical words for that work—atonement, propitiation, reconciliation, and redemption), the way in which the Holy Spirit applies the finished work of Christ to the individual, the church (what it is and how it should function), and the end of all things (particularly the final judgment, hell, and heaven).

We need specific powerful teaching about the Scriptures, the covenants, grace, the Law of God, election, effectual calling, justification, Christ's call to discipleship, and other doctrines. We do not hear preaching on these foundational truths very much today. This is a primary and debilitating weakness of the church.

But we also need a focus for going about this recovery, and the focus we chiefly need today is a renewed awareness of the reality and presence of God over against the preoccupation with man and his "felt needs" that has overwhelmed so many of our churches. There is a necessary balance here, of course. Theology involves both God and man, just as good preaching must speak to both the head and heart. But people tend to embrace extremes, and the pendulum today has certainly swung in the direction of an exclusively man-centered theology, worship, and church life. People come to church, if they do, with the question "What's in it for me?" and the tendency has been to reorder the message and life of the church to answer that question.

David F. Wells, professor of historical and systematic theology at Gordon-Conwell Theological Seminary, has analyzed this tendency in two good books: *No Place for Truth: Or Whatever Happened to Evangelical Theology?* and *God in the Wasteland: The Reality of Truth in a World of Fading Dreams.* In the second he writes, "The fundamental problem in the evangelical world today is not inadequate technique, insufficient organization, or antiquated music. . . . The fundamental problem in the evangelical world today is that God rests too inconsequentially upon the church. His truth is too distant, his grace too ordinary, his judgment is too benign, his gospel too easy, and his Christ too common."[1]

Clearly, in our day we need to push the pendulum back in the direction of a concern for God and his attributes and stress the doctrine of God again and again in our preaching.

But something else is needed. Ever since Immanuel Kant attacked the objective distinction between the self and the object to be known by the senses, perceiving the mind actually to form reality by the way it receives and analyzes external stimuli, the self has itself become the measure and determiner of all things, for Christians living in and formed by today's culture, as well as for others. Preoccupation with self is the chief sin of the modern world. And this means that without opposing the absorption with self, even a renewed effort to teach about God will be fruitless since it will end only by presenting a God to be used by us rather than a God who demands from us a surrender of self and radical obedience. We need to show that in the Bible God is not presented as an answer to our felt needs but as one who calls us to take up a cross daily and follow Jesus Christ.

Well says, "In a culture filled with [religious consumers], restoring weight to God is going to involve much more than simply getting some doctrine straight; it's going to entail a complete reconstruction of the modern self-absorbed pastiche personality."[2]

We may begin with a new examination of God's attributes.

1. *The sovereignty of God.* We can never exaggerate the importance of God's sovereignty, for God is the greatest of all realities, indeed, the very ground of reality, and sovereignty is the most important thing that can be said about him. The other attributes of God are

also important. But if, in our thinking, we should eliminate God's sovereignty, by which we mean the absolute determination and rule by God of all his works and creatures, God will no longer be God for us. His decrees and acts will be determined by something else, either by mere human beings or circumstances or some other cosmic power, and these other things (or nothing) will be our actual God.

In order to be sovereign God must also be all-knowing, all-powerful, and absolutely free. If he were limited in any one of these areas, he would not be truly sovereign. Yet the sovereignty of God is greater than any one of these or any other of the attributes it contains.

Sovereignty is no mere philosophical dogma, devoid of practical value. It is the one doctrine that gives meaning and substance to all the other doctrines. It is, as Arthur W. Pink observed, "the foundation of Christian theology . . . the center of gravity in the system of Christian truth—the sun around which all the lesser orbs are grouped."[3]

Thus far most evangelical Christians would probably agree, though they might feel that the sovereignty of God is not a very practical focus for Christian teaching today. But what we must also stress is the corollary doctrine to God's sovereignty, namely, that if God is sovereign over all things, then we are not, not even over the affairs of our personal lives. We are not in a position to determine what our lives should be or even what our true needs are, and we are certainly not to suppose even for an instant that the world revolves around ourselves.

If the doctrine of the sovereignty of God is to have clout in today's cultural setting, it must be opposed to the Nebuchadnezzar syndrome. In the fourth chapter of Daniel Nebuchadnezzar is standing on the roof of his palace, looking out over the magnificent city of Babylon with its glorious hanging gardens, and he is taking credit for what he sees. The text quotes him as boasting, "Is not this the great Babylon I have built as the royal residence, by my mighty power and for the glory of my majesty?" (v. 30). He is claiming that the world he observed was *of* him, *by* him, and *for* his glory.

That is the very essence of the world's spirit that exalts self in opposition to the sovereignty of the true God, and Nebuchadnezzar's boast may be the best single expression in all literature of what we today call secular humanism. But it is exactly that spirit that we see in today's evangelical churches as we construct bigger and bigger buildings and larger and larger ministries by catering to the love of self and by worldly means, rather than doing God's work by his might and in obedience to him.

In other words, the sovereignty of God more than any other single doctrine defines the essence of the struggle against the world and the flesh today. The struggle is over who is sovereign. Is it ourselves, perhaps the powerful of this world? Or is it the God of the Bible?

Fortunately, Nebuchadnezzar got the message. For his final testimony reads: "At the end of that time, I, Nebuchadnezzar, raised my eyes toward heaven, and my sanity was restored. Then I praised the Most High; I honored and glorified him who lives forever.

> His dominion is an eternal dominion;
> his kingdom endures from generation to generation.
> All the peoples of the earth
> are regarded as nothing.
> He does as he pleases
> with the powers of heaven
> and the peoples of the earth.
> No one can hold back his hand
> or say to him: "What have you done?"

. . . Now I, Nebuchadnezzar, praise and exalt and glorify the King of heaven, because everything he does is right and all his ways are just. And those who walk in pride he is able to humble" (vv. 34–37). God is not only *able* to humble them. He *does* humble them, and that is exactly what we need in the church today—especially we evangelicals.

2. The holiness of God. Sovereignty may be the most important of God's attributes, but if there is a rival to it, it is holiness. This is the attribute the Bible mentions most—not sovereignty or love, but holiness. "Who among the gods is like you, O LORD? Who is like you—majestic in holiness, awesome in glory, working wonders?" asked Moses (Exod. 15:11). When Isaiah had his vision of God he heard the seraphs crying,

> "Holy, holy, holy is the LORD Almighty;
> the whole earth is full of his glory" (Isa. 6:3).

In Revelation the four living creatures likewise cry out,

> "Holy, holy, holy
> is the Lord God Almighty,
> who was, and is, and is to come" (Rev. 4:8).

So also the saints who have been victorious over the beast and his image:

> "Who will not fear you, O Lord, and bring glory to your name? For you alone are holy" (Rev. 15:4).

Emil Brunner wrote, "From the standpoint of revelation the first thing which has to be said about God is his sovereignty. But this first point is intimately connected with a second—so closely indeed that we might even ask whether it ought not to have come first: God is the holy one."[4]

But today? God's holiness weighs "lightly upon us," says Wells.[5] Why? One problem is that the holiness of God is difficult to understand, and evangelicals along with others certainly do not understand it. It is not just a question of morality, as if all we are saying when we say that God is holy is that he is always right in what he does. Holiness involves God's transcendence, what makes him *ganz anders,* as the German theologians say. It involves majesty, the authority of sovereign power, stateliness, or grandeur. It embraces the idea of God's sovereign majestic will, a will that is set upon proclaiming himself to be who he truly is: God alone, who will not allow his glory to be diminished by another.

Yet failing to understand what the holiness of God means is only one problem, and a lesser one at that. A far greater problem is that the holiness of God is something of which human beings must stand in awe, and there is very little about which people today do stand in awe, least of all God. We live in an age when everything is exposed, where there are no mysteries and no surprises, where even the most intimate personal secrets of our lives are blurted out over television to entertain the masses. We are contributing to this frivolity when we treat God as our celestial buddy who indulges us in the banalities of our day-to-day lives.

Perhaps the greatest problem of all in regard to our neglect of God's holiness is that holiness is a standard against which human sin is exposed, which is why in Scripture exposure to God always produces feelings of shame, guilt, embarrassment, and terror in the worshiper. These are all painful emotions, and we are doing everything possible in our culture to avoid them. One evidence of this is the way we have eliminated sin as a serious category for describing human actions. Karl Menninger, founder of the world famous Menninger Clinic in Topeka, Kansas, asked *Whatever Became of Sin?*[6] and answered that by banishing God from our cultural landscape we have changed sin into crime (because it is now no longer an offense against God, which is what sin is, but rather an offense against the state) and then have changed crime into symptoms. Sin is now something that is someone else's fault. It is caused by my environment, my parents, or my genes.

Menninger suggests that psychiatrists may have compounded the problem by "neglecting the availability of help for some individuals whose sins are greater than their symptoms and whose burdens are greater than they can bear."[7] This is what evangelicals have done, too. We, too, have bought into today's therapeutic culture so that we no longer call our many transgressions sin or confront sin directly, calling for repentance before God. Instead we send our people to counselors to work through why they are acting in an "unhealthy" manner, to find "healing."

David Wells claims that "holiness fundamentally defines the character of God." But "robbed of such a God, worship loses its awe, the truth of his Word loses its ability to compel, obedience loses its virtue, and the church loses its moral authority."[8] It is time for evangelical churches to recover the Bible's insistence that God is holy above all things and to explore what that must mean for our indi-

God's Love will / Cannot reach His Justice (handwritten annotation)

vidual and corporate lives. To begin with we need to preach from those great passages of the Bible in which people were exposed to God's awe-inspiring majesty and holiness. If nothing else, we need to preach the Law without which preaching the gospel loses its power and eventually even its meaning.

3. *The wisdom of God.* What do we mean when we say that God is wise or all-wise? We mean that God is omniscient, of course. God could not be all-wise unless he were all-knowing. But wisdom is more than mere knowledge, more even than total or perfect knowledge. A person can have a great deal of knowledge—we call it "head knowledge"—and not know what to do with it. He can know a great deal about a lot of things and still be a fool. And there is the matter of goodness too. Without goodness, wisdom is not wisdom. Rather it is what we call cunning. Wisdom consists in knowing what to do with the knowledge one has and with directing that knowledge to the highest and most moral ends.

Charles Hodge says that God's wisdom is seen "in the selection of proper ends and of proper means for the accomplishment of those ends."[9]

J. I. Packer says the same thing but emphasizes goodness. "Wisdom is the power to see, and the inclination to choose, the best and highest goal, together with the surest means of attaining it. Wisdom is, in fact, the practical side of moral goodness. As such, it is found in its fullness only in God. He alone is naturally and entirely and invariably wise. . . . Wisdom, as the old theologians used to say, is his *essence,* just as power and truth and goodness are his *essence*— integral elements, that is, in his character. . . . Omniscience governing omnipotence, infinite power ruled by infinite wisdom, is a biblical description of the divine character."[10]

As soon as we begin to think along these lines we see at once why our human wisdom does not begin to compare with God's and why Paul can say, as he does in writing to the Corinthians, "Where is the wise man? Where is the scholar? Where is the philosopher of this age? Has not God made foolish the wisdom of the world? For since in the wisdom of God the world through its wisdom did not know him, God was pleased through the foolishness of what was preached to save those who believe" (1 Cor. 1:20–21).

Grace or works dilemma

We need to be amazed and humbled by God's wisdom once again. Here are three areas in which this needs to happen.

First, *the wisdom of God in justification.* The first main section of Romans (chaps. 1–4) asks how God, who is a God of perfect justice and must punish sin, is nevertheless able to save sinners. This is *the* question of all questions. The answer is beyond the wisdom of mere men and women. But it was not beyond the wisdom of God. Thus, in the fullness of time "God sent his Son, born of a woman, born under the law, to redeem those under the law, that we might receive the full rights of sons" (Gal. 4:4–5). Or, to use Paul's language in Romans: "God presented him as a sacrifice of atonement . . . to demonstrate his justice at the present time." God satisfied the claims of his justice by punishing Jesus in our place. Thus, the demands of God's justice were fully met and, justice being satisfied, the love of God was free to reach out, embrace, and fully save the sinner.

Who but God could think up a solution to that problem? None of us could have done it, but God fit the most perfect means to the most desirable of ends and so saved sinners.

Second, *the wisdom of God in sanctification.* The next major section of Romans (chaps. 5–8) discusses the permanent nature of salvation, embracing the sinner's need for sanctification. How is the wisdom of God revealed in this area? The justification discussed in chapters 1–4 is provided by the work of Christ, which means that it is not of ourselves. It is of grace. But if that is so, what is to stop a justified person from indulging in his or her sinful nature, since the person's salvation has already been secured by Christ's work? There seems to be no need for holiness (Rom. 6:1).

We are caught on the horns of a dilemma. Either salvation must be by works, which destroys grace, besides which no one would be saved, since none can provide sufficient good works. Or else, if salvation is of grace, then we must be free to sin greatly.

God solves this problem by showing that we are never justified apart from being regenerated or being made alive in Christ. Christians have been given a new nature, and this new nature, being the very life of Jesus Christ within, will inevitably produce good works corresponding to the character of God. In fact, this is the only sure proof of our having been saved by him. Moreover, since this is the work of God, not our work, we cannot undo it and so somehow go back to being what we were before. Since we can't go back, the only way we can move on is forward. Paul's way of saying this is a forceful imperative: "In the same way, count yourselves dead to sin but alive to God in Christ Jesus" (Rom. 6:11).

Who but God could think up a gospel like that? We never would, because we do not naturally hold grace and works together. If we emphasize morality, as some persons do, we begin to think that we can be saved by our good works and so strive to do it. We repudiate grace. But if, on the other hand, we emphasize grace, knowing that we cannot possibly be saved by our inadequate and polluted works, we tend to do away with works entirely and so slide into antinomianism. But God has devised a gospel that is entirely, completely of grace and yet produces the most exceptional works in those who are saved.

Third, *the wisdom of God in history.* The third section of Romans (chaps. 9–11) is concerned with the acts of God in the flow of historical events. As Paul describes it, the problem is that although God made great salvation promises to the Jewish people, in spite of these promises, the majority of Jews were not responding to the gospel. Doesn't this indicate that the purposes of God have failed? And what about the Gentiles? In Paul's day Gentiles seemed to be responding to the gospel. Does this mean that God has rejected the Jews in favor of the Gentiles? If he has, isn't that wrong? And doesn't it destroy the doctrine of eternal security?

Paul's answer is a magnificent theodicy in which he justifies the ways of God with men, showing that God has rejected Israel for a time in order that his mercy might be extended to the Gentiles, but adding that Gentile salvation will provoke Israel to jealousy and so in time bring the Jewish people to faith in Jesus as the Messiah. These chapters are an exploration of the wisdom of God in the ordering of space/time events.

Who could devise a plan of that scope for world history? We could not do it. We can only understand it on the basis of the biblical revelation, and even then it is difficult for us. But it is not beyond "the depth of the riches of the wisdom . . . of God" (Rom. 11:33).

God's wisdom ⟷ our wisdom

This wisdom of God is so much superior to our wisdom that it may hardly be compared to it. Yet the Bible encourages us to cultivate wisdom. Ephesians 5:17 says, "Do not be foolish, but understand what the Lord's will is." James, the Lord's brother, promises, "If any of you lacks wisdom, he should ask God, who gives generously to all without finding fault, and it will be given to him" (James 1:5).

How may wisdom be found? The answer is: (1) begin with reverence for God (Prov. 9:10 says, "The fear of the LORD is the beginning of wisdom"); (2) study to know God's Word, the Bible (Paul told Timothy that the Scriptures "are able to make you wise for salvation through faith in Christ Jesus," 2 Tim. 3:15); and (3) ask God for it (James 1:5). Especially study the Bible! The true church has always drawn its life and found its sure direction from the Bible. In fact, severed from the Bible the church is no longer able to be the church, though it may continue to behave in churchly ways and do religious things.

If we really believed that God is all-wise and if we really wanted to be wise ourselves, we would seek God's wisdom in the Bible—fervently and consistently. We would study to be wise. But we do not really believe in God's wisdom. Martin Luther said, "We are accustomed to admit freely that God is more powerful than we are, but not that he is wiser than we are. To be sure, we say that he is; but when it comes to a showdown, we do not want to act on what we say."[11]

Reformation in Worship

John R. W. Stott has written a book on "some essentials of evangelical religion" in which he affirms "that true worship is the highest and noblest activity of which man, by the grace of God, is capable."[12] But that highlights our weakness, namely, that for large segments of the evangelical church, perhaps the majority, true worship is almost non-existent.

A. W. Tozer, a wise pastor and perceptive Bible student, saw the problem nearly fifty years ago. He wrote in 1948, "Thanks to our splendid Bible societies and to other effective agencies for the dissemination of the Word, there are today many millions of people who hold 'right opinions,' probably more than ever before in the history of the church. Yet I wonder if there was ever a time when true spiritual worship was at a lower ebb. To great sections of the church the art of worship has been lost entirely, and in its place has come that strange and foreign thing called the 'program.' This word has been borrowed from the stage and applied with sad wisdom to the type of public service which now passes for worship among us."[13]

1. *Christian worship.* It is not unusual to read in books dealing with worship that worship is hard to define, but I do not find that actually to be the case. I think it is very easy to define. The problems—and there are many of them—are in different areas.

def

To worship God is to ascribe to him supreme worth, for he alone is supremely worthy. Therefore, the first thing to be said about worship is that it is to honor God. Worship also has bearing on the worshiper. It changes him or her, which is the second important thing to be said about it. William Temple defined worship very well: "To worship is to quicken the conscience by the holiness of God, to feed the mind with the truth of God, to purge the imagination by the beauty of God, to open the heart to the love of God, to devote the will to the purpose of God."[14]

In that definition the attributes of God are foremost: holiness, truth, beauty and love, and also God's purposes. But these, rightly acknowledged and praised, impact the worshiper by quickening the conscience, feeding the mind, purging the imagination, opening the heart, and devoting (or winning) the will. Thus, in defining worship, William Temple also gave us a description of the true Christian life and defined godliness.

2. *Contemporary "worship."* John H. Armstrong is editor of a journal called *Reformation and Revival,* and he devoted the 1993 winter issue to worship. In the introduction Armstrong calls what passes for the worship of God today "Mac-Worship," meaning that worship has been made common, cheap, or trivial. What is the problem? Why is so little of that strong worship that characterized past ages seen among us? There are several reasons.

First, *ours is a trivial age,* and the church has been deeply affected by this pervasive triviality. Ours is not an age for great thoughts or even great actions. Our age has no heroes. It is a technological age, and the ultimate objective of our popular technological culture is entertainment.

In recent years I have been holding seminars in various parts of the country on the subject of developing a Christian mind, and I have a written a small book on the same subject, based on Romans 12:1–2, called *Mind Renewal in a Mindless Age.* In those seminars and in the book, I argue that the chief (though not the only cause) of today's mindlessness is television, which is not a teaching or informing medium, as most people suppose, it is but rather a means of entertainment. Because it is so pervasive—the average American household has the television on more than seven hours a day—it is programming us to think that the chief end of man is to be entertained. How can people whose minds are filled with the brainless babble of the evening sitcoms have anything but trivial thoughts when they come to God's house on Sunday mornings if, in fact, they have thoughts of God at all? How can they appreciate his holiness if their heads are full of the moral muck of the afternoon talk shows? All they can look for in church, if they look for anything, is something to make them feel good for a short while before they go back to the television culture.

Second, *ours is a self-absorbed, man-centered age,* and the church has become sadly, even treasonously, self-centered. We have seen something like a "Copernican Revolution" in the evangelical church's understanding of worship in this area in our lifetimes. In the past, as in Tozer's day, true worship may not have taken place all the time or even often. It may have been crowded out by the "program," as Tozer maintained it was in his day. But worship was at least understood to be the praise of God and to be something worth aiming at. Today we do not even aim at it, at least not much or in many places.

Pastor R. Kent Hughes, senior pastor of the College Church in Wheaton, is on target when he says, "The unspoken but increasingly common assumption of today's Christendom is that worship is primarily for *us*—to meet our needs. Such worship services are entertainment focused, and the worshipers are uncommitted spectators who are silently grading the performance. From this perspective preaching becomes a homiletics of consensus—preaching to felt needs—man's conscious agenda instead of God's. Such preaching is always topical and never textual. Biblical information is minimized, and the sermons are short and full of stories. Anything and everything that is suspected of making the marginal attender uncomfortable is removed from the service, whether it be a registration card or a 'mere' creed. Taken to the nth degree, this philosophy instills a tragic self-centeredness. That is, everything is judged by how it affects man. This terribly corrupts one's theology."[15]

Third, *we are oblivious to God.* The tragedy is not that we deny basic Bible doctrines, certainly not the nature and existence of God. Evangelicals are not heretics. The problem is that although we acknowledge Bible truth, it seems to make no difference. It has no bearing on us.

In recent years, as I have traveled around the country speaking in various churches, I have noticed the decreasing presence and in some cases the total absence of service elements that have always been associated with the worship of God. These desperately need to be recovered.

Prayer. It is almost inconceivable to me that something that is called a worship service can be held without any significant prayer, but that is precisely what is happening. There is usually a very short prayer at the beginning of the service and another prayer at the time the offering is received. But longer prayers, pastoral prayers, are vanishing. Whatever happened to the ACTS acrostic in which "A" stands for adoration, "C" for confession of sin, "T" for thanksgiving, and "S" for supplication? Now and then a few supplications are tacked onto the offering prayer. But there is no rehearsal of God's attributes or confession of sin over against a serious acknowledgment that God is holy. How can we say we are worshiping when we do not even pray?

The reading of the Word. The reading of any substantial portion of the Bible is also vanishing. In the Puritan age ministers regularly read one long chapter of the Old Testament and one chapter of the New Testament. But our Scripture readings are getting shorter and shorter, sometimes only two or three verses, if indeed the Bible is read at all. In many churches there is not even a text for the sermon.

The exposition of the Word. And what about sermons? We have very little serious teaching of the Bible today. Instead, preachers try to be personable, to relate funny stories, to smile, above all to stay away from topics that might cause people to become unhappy with the church and leave it. One extremely popular television preacher will not talk about sin on the grounds that doing so makes people feel bad. Preachers are to preach to felt needs, not real needs necessarily, and this generally means telling people only what they want to hear. Preachers want to be liked. They want to be entertaining. Was Jesus liked? Were Martin Luther, John Calvin, John Wesley, or Jonathan Edwards entertainers?

Confession of sin. Who confesses sin today—anywhere, not to mention in church as God's humble, repentant people? It is not happening, because there is so little awareness of God. Instead of coming to church to admit our transgressions and seek forgiveness, we come to church to be told that we are really all right and do not need forgiveness.

Hymns. One of the saddest features of contemporary worship is that the great hymns of the church are on the way out. They are not gone entirely, but they are going. And in their place have come trite jingles that have more in common with contemporary advertising ditties than the psalms. The problem here is not so much the style of the music, though trite words fit best with trite tunes and harmonies. Rather it is with the content of the songs. The old hymns expressed the theology of the church in profound and perceptive ways and with winsome, memorable language. Today's songs reflect only our shallow or non-existent theology and do almost nothing to elevate our thoughts about God.

Worst of all are songs that merely repeat a trite idea, word, or phrase over and over again. Songs like this are not worship, though they may give the churchgoer a religious feeling. They are mantras, which belong more in a gathering of New Agers than among the worshiping people of God.

3. *Rediscovering worship.* The disaster that has overtaken the church in our day in regard to worship is not going to be remedied overnight. But we ought to make a start, and one way to begin is to study what Jesus said about worship. He had been traveling with

his disciples and had stopped at the well of Sychar while the disciples went into the city to buy food. A woman came to draw water and Jesus got into a discussion with her. As the discussion progressed he touched on her loose moral life, revealing his insight into her way of living, and she tried to change the topic by asking him a religious question. "Sir," she said, "I can see that you are a prophet. Our fathers worshiped on this mountain, but you Jews claim that the place where we must worship is in Jerusalem" (John 4:19–20).

Jesus' answer is the classic biblical statement of what worship is all about: "Believe me, woman, a time is coming when you will worship the Father neither on this mountain nor in Jerusalem. You Samaritans worship what you do not know; we worship what we do know, for salvation is from the Jews. Yet a time is coming and has now come when the true worshipers will worship the Father in spirit and truth, for they are the kind of worshipers the Father seeks. God is spirit, and his worshipers must worship in spirit and in truth" (vv. 21–24). There are several important things about what Jesus said.

First, *there is but one true God, and true worship must be of this true God and none other.* This is the point of Jesus saying that the Samaritans did not know who they were worshiping but that the Jews did, that "salvation is from the Jews." He meant that the true God is the God who had revealed himself to Israel at Mount Sinai and who established the only acceptable way of worshiping him, which is what much of the Old Testament is about. Other worship is invalid, because it is worship of an imaginary god.

We need to think about this carefully because we live in an age in which everyone's opinion about anything, especially his or her opinion about God, is thought to be as valid as any other. That is patently impossible. If there is a God, which is basic to any discussion about worship, then God is what he is. That is, he is one thing and not another. So the question is not whether any or all opinions are valid but rather what this one true existing God is like. Who is he? What is his name? What kind of a God is he? Christianity teaches that this one true God has made himself known through creation, at Mount Sinai, through the subsequent history of the Jewish people, and in the incarnation, life, death, and resurrection of his

Son Jesus Christ. In addition, he has given us a definitive revelation of what he is like and what he requires of us in the Bible. That is the point at which we start. There is one God, and he has revealed himself to us. That is why there can be no true worship of God without a faithful teaching of the Bible.

Second, *the only way this one true God can be truly worshiped is "in spirit and in truth."* Jesus was indicating a change in dispensations when he said this. Before this time worship was centered in the temple at Jerusalem. Every Jew had to make his way there three times annually for the festivals. What took place in the local synagogues was more like a Bible school class than a worship service. But this has been changed. Jesus has come. He has fulfilled all the temple worship symbolized. Therefore, until the end of the new church age worship is not to be by location, either in Jerusalem or Samaria, but in spirit and according to the truth of God.

Worship should not be confused with feelings. It is true that the worship of God will affect us, and one thing it will frequently affect is our emotions. At times tears will fill our eyes as we become aware of God's great love and grace toward us. Yet it is possible for our eyes to fill with tears and for there still to be no real worship simply because we have not come to a genuine awareness of God and a fuller praise of himself in his nature and ways.

True worship occurs only when that part of man, his spirit, which is akin to the divine nature (for God is spirit), actually meets with God and finds itself praising God for his love, wisdom, beauty, truth, holiness, compassion, mercy, grace, power, and all his other attributes.

William Barclay has written: "The true, the genuine worship is when man, through his spirit, attains to friendship and intimacy with God. True and genuine worship is not to come to a certain place; it is not to go through a certain ritual or liturgy; it is not even to bring certain gifts. True worship is when the spirit, the immortal and invisible part of man, speaks to and meets with God, who is immortal and invisible."[16]

4. *Is liturgy good or bad?* The fact that we are to worship God "in spirit" also has bearing on the various types of liturgy used in Christian churches, for it means that, with the exception of elements that

suggest wrong doctrine, there is no liturgy that in itself is inherently better or worse than another. For any given congregation, one type of service will presumably be more valuable than another at directing the attention of the worshipers to God. But the decision as to what that type of service will be ought to be arrived at, not by asking whether one prefers contemporary or traditional music, extemporaneous or read prayers, congregational responses or silence—in short, whether one prefers Anglican, Lutheran, Presbyterian, Methodist, Baptist, Congregational, or Quaker services—but by asking how effective the service is in turning the attention of the worshiper away from the service itself to God. In this respect an order of worship is to be evaluated on the same basis that we ought to evaluate the preacher.

In thinking through this particular issue I have been helped by C. S. Lewis. Lewis was a member of the Church of England and was accustomed to various forms of what we might call a formal service. But he did not plead for formality. He asked merely for what he called "uniformity" on the grounds that novelty at best directs our attention to the novelty and at the worst turns it to the one who is enacting the liturgy. This is a point at which many contemporary services fail dreadfully, in my judgment. They are trying to be so "creative" that the attender goes away impressed only with the novelty of what has been going on.

Lewis wrote, "As long as you notice, and have to count, the steps, you are not yet dancing but only learning to dance. A good shoe is a shoe you don't have to notice. Good reading becomes possible when you need not consciously think about eyes, or light, or print, or spelling. The perfect church service would be one we were almost unaware of; our attention would have been on God."[17]

The wonder of Christian worship is that when we come to God in the way he has established, we find him to be inexhaustible and discover that our desire to know and worship him further is increased. Bernard of Clairvaux knew this. He wrote toward the middle of the twelfth century:

> Jesus, thou Joy of loving hearts,
> Thou Fount of life, thou Light of men,
> From the best bliss that earth imparts

We turn unfilled to thee again.
We taste thee, O thou living Bread,
And long to feast upon thee still;
We drink of thee, the Fountainhead,
And thirst our souls from thee to fill.

When we worship in that way we find ourselves approaching what the compilers of the Westminster Shorter Catechism rightly called the chief end of man. "What is the chief end of man?" The catechism answers, "Man's chief end is to glorify God, and to enjoy him forever."

Reformation in Life

Surveys of contemporary Christian conduct tell us that most Christians do not act significantly different from non-Christian people. This is not surprising since little contemporary preaching teaches about or encourages a difference. But we obviously should be different, at least if we take the Bible seriously. Christians are to be the new humanity, a community of those who "love . . . God, even to the contempt of self" as opposed to those who "love . . . self, even to the contempt of God."[18]

Where should we start? The scope of this subject is analogous to that of the reformation of the church in doctrine with which this chapter began. I asked what doctrines needed to be recovered, and I answered "all the major doctrines of all the creeds." Here I ask, What areas of Christian life and conduct need to be recovered? The answer is: all areas of life both for ourselves as individuals and the church. We need the Ten Commandments, the Sermon on the Mount, and the ethical teaching of the Epistles. It is all needed. In short, we need to recover what it means to "love the Lord your God with all your heart and with all your soul and with all your mind" and to "love your neighbor as yourself" since "all the Law and the Prophets hang on these two commandments" (Matt. 22:37–40).

But again, we need a focus. We most need to recover an awareness of those spiritual realities that are invisible, that is, not seen or measured like other merely material things, and the reality of Christian community.

1. *Things that are invisible.* In 2 Corinthians Paul explains why, although opposition to the gospel is great outwardly and he and the other leaders of the early church are wasting away under the constant duties and pressures of the ministry, he does not get defeated or discouraged. It is because "our light and momentary troubles are achieving for us an eternal glory that far outweighs them all. So we fix our eyes not on what is seen, but on what is unseen. For what is seen is temporary, but what is unseen is eternal" (2 Cor. 4:17–18).

What has happened to many segments of the evangelical church is that we have forgotten to focus on that which is eternal. Too much attention is being paid to growing large congregations, increasing already enormous budgets, erecting ever more elaborate buildings, and gaining more and more recognition from the world, and not enough attention to what really matters, namely, God himself, truth, spiritual rebirth, holiness in church members, and glorifying God in our doctrine, worship, and church life.

Abraham is the outstanding biblical example of those who live by faith in God, having their eyes set on what is invisible rather than what can be seen. Thus in Hebrews 11 he is brought forward as a hero of faith, one who "looked for a city with foundations," that is, God's city, rather than an earthly city with earthly foundations that will pass away. The first words about Abraham in Hebrews 11 say, "By faith Abraham, when called to go to a place he would later receive as his inheritance, obeyed and went, even though he did not know where he was going. By faith he made his home in the promised land like a stranger in a foreign country; he lived in tents, as did Isaac and Jacob, who were heirs with him of the same promise. For he was looking forward to the city with foundations, whose architect and builder is God" (vv. 8–10).

It is only people who live with their eyes on what is unseen who ultimately make any real difference in the world.

2. *Christian community.* The second great need in our day is that the church become a genuine community—community, because it is only as a community that we can model relationships; Christian, because what we want to model is the unique qualities of life that

being Christians brings. The great twentieth-century English poet T. S. Eliot asked:

> When the Stranger says, "What is the meaning of this city?
> Do you huddle close together because you love each other?"
> What will you answer? "We all dwell together
> To make money from each other" or "This is a community"?
>
> (Chorus from "The Rock")

Anthony T. Evans is a successful black pastor in Dallas, Texas. He is an excellent Bible expositor, and his goal is to have the great population centers of America experience spiritual renewal. Evans publishes a monthly newsletter called *The Urban Alternative* in which there appeared an article entitled "10 Steps to Urban Renewal." It mentioned sound Bible teaching, rejection of government dependence, use of spiritual gifts, the discipling of converts, and other such things. One important requirement, according to Evans, is becoming a community. He wrote, "The church is first and foremost a spiritual family, a community. That's why the Bible refers to the church as a 'household of faith,' 'family of God' and 'brothers and sisters.' It's meant to function as a family, model family life, and care for the families it encompasses."[19]

The church can do that as no other organization can—not businesses, not schools, not the centers of entertainment or social life, not government or city agencies. Only the church! Besides, churches have an extraordinary opportunity to model community at a time when other forms of community have broken down. There is no better place than the fellowship of Christians for embracing those suffering from ruptured marriages, fractured homes, and other destroyed relationships.

The world is looking for community, even though it may not know it and usually does not seek it in the church. Since the 1970s there have been two major changes in the way Americans look at other people and relate to them: (1) Our present-day mechanized society treats people as things that have a function, rather than as people with a purpose; and (2) we have become preoccupied with

An outlook that defines self will destroy the self.

ourselves, rather than seeing ourselves in community with and existing to help other people.

This has been noted by secular observers. In *The Greening of America* Charles Reich wrote, "America is one vast, terrifying anti-community. . . . Modern living has obliterated place, locality, and neighborhood, and given us the anonymous separateness of our existence. The family, the most basic social system, has been ruthlessly stripped to its functional essentials. Friendship has been coated over with a layer of impenetrable artificiality as men strive to live roles designed for them. Protocol, competition, hostility, and fear have replaced the warmth of the circle of affection which might sustain man against a hostile universe."[20]

Christianity has something to offer at this point. God said, "It is not good for the man to be alone" (Gen. 2:18). Jesus said, "I will build my church" (Matt. 16:18). In Acts 2 we are told of the early believers, "They devoted themselves to the apostles' teaching and to *the fellowship,* to the breaking of bread and to prayer" (Acts 2:42).

We need to recover this. Michael Scott Horton has written rightly, "Our churches are one of the last bastions of community, and yet, they do not escape individualism. . . . Many of us drive to church, listen to the sermon, say 'hello' to our circle of friends, and return home without ever having really experienced community. Earlier evangelicalism was so focused on corporate spirituality that communion was taken with a common cup. . . . We hear endless sermons on spiritual gifts and how the body of Christ is supposed to operate in concert. And yet, our services often are made up of the professionals (particularly the choir) who entertain us and the individual, separate believers who are entertained."[21]

There are several important implications of the biblical emphasis on community. First, people are more important than programs. Programs should serve people rather than it being the other way around. Second, we must think about other people rather than ourselves all the time. Evangelicals must stop asking, "What's in it for me?" and start asking, "How can I help the other person?" An outlook that deifies self will destroy the self. Concentrating on other people is the best way to find happiness.

What makes a community? A community holds together only by some higher allegiance or priority, and the only adequate base for real community among people is devotion to God. Christians have a commitment that goes beyond mere individualism, or at least they should, and if they do, they can model community in a church setting. Moreover, if they can do it there, they can begin to model it in other environments.

To God Alone Be Glory

This chapter began with God, and it is appropriate that it end with God, too, for a recovery of the sense of the reality, presence, will, and glory of God is what it is about. Earlier I wrote about the Apostle Paul's handling of justification, sanctification, and a biblical view of history in Romans 1–11. It is significant that this great doctrinal section of the letter ends with a doxology. The last words are:

> For from him and through him and to him are all things,
> To him be the glory forever! Amen (Rom. 11:36).

Moreover, after the closing application section of the letter, the entire Epistle ends similarly: "To the only wise God be glory forever through Jesus Christ! Amen" (Rom. 16:27).

I would argue that the reason the evangelical church is so weak today and why we do not experience renewal, though we talk about our need for it, is that the glory of God has been largely forgotten by the church. We are not likely to see revival again until the truths that exalt and glorify God in salvation are recovered. How can we expect God to move among us until we can again truthfully say, "To God alone be the glory"?

The world cannot say this. It is concerned for its own glory instead. Like Nebuchadnezzar, it says, "Look at this great Babylon I have built by my power and for my glory." Arminians cannot say it. They can say, "to God be glory," but they cannot say, "to God *alone* be glory" since Arminian theology takes some of the glory of God in salvation and gives it to an individual who has the final say in whether or not he or she will be saved. Even those in the Reformed camp cannot say it if what they are chiefly trying to do in their ministries is build their own kingdoms and became important people on the religious scene. We will never experience renewal in doctrine, worship, and life until we are able honestly to say, "to God *alone* be glory."

To those who do not know God that is perhaps the most foolish of all statements. But to those who do know God, to those who are being saved, it is not only a right statement; it is a happy, true, inescapable, necessary, and highly desirable confession.

Notes

Chapter 1: David F. Wells

1. Robert H. Bork, "The Hard Truth about America," *The Christian Activist* 7 (October 1995): 1.

2. William J. Bennett, *The Index of Leading Cultural Indicators* (Washington: The Heritage Foundation, 1993), 3.

3. Ibid., 10.

4. Ibid., 13.

5. Ibid., 23.

6. James Patterson and Peter Kim, *The Day America Told the Truth: What People Really Believe about Everything That Matters* (New York: Prentice Hall, 1991), 27.

7. Ibid.

8. Ibid., 48, 57.

9. This is the central theme pursued in Arthur A. Schlesinger's *The Disuniting of America: Reflections on a Multicultural Society* (New York: Norton, 1993).

10. This double rejection of absolute morality and absolute truth is not without significance when it is recalled that the Bible also links these two matters. Truth is the opposite both of what is intellectually false and of what is morally defiled. This yoking of belief and behavior, what is true and what is right, in the biblical understanding of truth is perhaps nowhere more succinctly stated than in John's words: "If we claim to have fellowship with him [God] yet walk in the [moral] darkness, we lie and do not live by the truth" (1 John 1:6). See also John 1:4, 5, 9; 3:19–21; 7:18; 8:12; 12:35, 36, 40; Eph. 4:25; 1 John 2:8–11, 27.

11. Camille Paglia, *Sex, Art, and American Culture* (New York: Vintage, 1992), vii.

12. Ibid., 102.

13. Camille Paglia, *Vamps and Tramps: New Essays* (New York: Vintage, 1994), 20.

14. Ibid., 66.

15. At this conference goddess worship in the form of Sophia occurred and in a ritual involving the elements of milk and honey the following prayer was offered: "Our maker Sophia, we are women in your image: With the hot blood of our wombs we give form to new life. . . . Our sweet Sophia, we are women in your image: with nectar between our thighs we invite a lover, we birth a child; with our warm body fluids we remind the world of its pleasures and sensations. . . . With the honey of wisdom in our mouths, we prophesy a full humanity to all the peoples."

16. Carl E. Braaten and Robert Jenson, eds., *Either/Or: The Gospel or Neopaganism* (Grand Rapids: Eerdmans, 1995); see also Peter Jones, *Spirit Wars: The Revival of Paganism on the Threshold of the 3rd Millennium* (Nashville: Thomas Nelson, 1995).

17. John Silber, "Obedience to the Unenforceable," unpublished address, Boston University, 1995, 2. Silber's brief discussion of the three domains is, for my purposes here, more helpful than that typical threefold division of private, public, and voluntary associations.

18. This distinction runs throughout Robert N. Bellah, Richard Madsen, William M. Sullivan, Ann Swidler, and

Steven M. Tipton, *Habits of the Heart: Individualism and Commitment in American Life* (New York: Harper and Row, 1985).

19. Bellah, *The Good Society*, 44.

20. Zbigniew Brzezinski, *Out of Control: Global Turmoil on the Eve of the Twenty-First Century* (New York: Charles Scribner's Sons, 1993), 65.

21. Bellah, *The Good Society*, 83.

22. David Riesman, "On Autonomy," in *The Self in Social Interaction,* ed. Chad Gordon and Kenneth Gerge (New York: Wiley, 1968), 446. I have also attempted to sketch out how our individualism has developed and why it is now so problematic in my *No Place for Truth: Or Whatever Happened to Evangelical Theology?* (Grand Rapids: Eerdmans, 1993), 149–86.

23. Normally, the discovery of unhappy moral realities lying behind the image might diminish the prospects of success for a performer. But not always. In our culture there are some deep pools of perversity that produce the opposite result. In 1993, for example, rapper Snoop Doggy Dogg was charged with murder in a drive-by shooting. His debut as a rapper that year was in an album called "Doggystyle." Despite the murder charge—or, more correctly, because of it— the album made history by rising to the top of the charts the first week it was out.

24. Dick Keyes, *True Heroism: In a World of Celebrity Counterfeits* (Colorado Springs: Navpress, 1995), 14–16; see also Joshua Gamsun, *Claims to Fame: Celebrity in Contemporary America* (Berkeley: University of California Press, 1994).

25. Daniel J. Boorstin, *The Image; or, What Happened to the American Dream* (New York: Atheneum, 1962), 61.

26. John Leo, "Decadence, the Corporate Way," *U.S. News and World Report*, August 28–September 4, 1995, 31.

27. Andrew Delbanco, *The Death of Satan: How Americans Have Lost the Sense of Evil* (New York: Farrar, Straus and Giroux, 1995), 153.

28. Ibid., 188.

29. Ibid., 221. John Diggins has recognized the consequences of this in our hollowed out political life and has sought to retrieve from the Founding Fathers and from subsequent thinkers those values and beliefs which, if reaffirmed, might restore some authority to our political order. See his *The Lost Soul of American Politics: Virtue, Self-Interest, and the Foundations of Liberalism* (New York: Basic, 1984). Others have moved in a different, more religious direction. Robert Wuthnow has suggested that civil religion now has two forms, one that articulates the goals of the political Left and the other of the political Right. "On the conservative side, America's legitimacy seems to depend heavily on a distinct 'myth of origin' that relates the nation's founding to divine purposes." This is what gives America a special place in the world and a certain divine approval to its foreign policy initiatives. The liberal view of America does not root its interest in America's founding under God. It argues that America has a role to play in the world, not because it is some kind of chosen people, but because of the ethical responsibility that follows upon its position of power and its wealth in the world today. "Rather than drawing specific attention to the distinctiveness of the Judeo-Christian tradition, liberal civil religion is much more likely to include arguments about basic human rights and common human problems" (Robert Wuthnow, *The Restructuring of American Religion: Society and Faith Since World War II* [Princeton: Princeton University Press, 1988], 244, 250). Both forms of civil religion, however, miscarry for neither adequately and convincingly can shore up the fallen middle between law and freedom. See also Robert Wuthnow, *The Struggle for America's Soul: Evangelicals, Liberals, and Secularism* (Grand Rapids: Eerdmans, 1989), 97–114.

30. Gregory C. Sisk, "The Moral Incompetence of the Judiciary," *First Things* 57 (November 1995): 34.

31. Roderick MacLeish, "Is Litigation Becoming an American Pastime?" *The Boston Globe* (March 8, 1996), 23, 27.

32. Richard Bernstein, *Dictatorship of Virtue: Multiculturalism and the Battle for America's Future* (New York: Knopf, 1994).

33. See Dinesh D'Souza, *Illiberal Education: The Politics of Race and Sex on Campus* (New York: The Free Press, 1991).

34. Charles J. Sykes, *A Nation of Victims: The Decay of the American Character* (New York: St. Martin's, 1992), 11.

Chapter 3: R. Albert Mohler Jr.

1. Brian Hebblethwaite, *The Ocean of Truth: A Defense of Objective Theism* (Cambridge: Cambridge University Press, 1988), 17.

2. Scott Cowdell, *Atheist Priest? Don Cupitt and Christianity* (London: SCM, 1988).

3. Don Cupitt, *Taking Leave of God* (New York: Crossroad, 1981).

4. Eric Hobsbawm, *The Age of Extremes: A History of the World, 1914–1991* (New York: Pantheon, 1995).

5. See R. Albert Mohler Jr., "The Integrity of the Evangelical Tradition and the Challenge of the Postmodern Paradigm," in *The Challenge of Postmodernism: An Evangelical Engagement,* ed. David S. Dockery (Wheaton, Ill.: Bridgepoint, 1995), 67–88.

6. Matei Calinescu, *Five Faces of Modernity* (Durham, N.C.: Duke University Press, 1987), 64.

7. See Dean R. Hoge, Benton Johnson, and Donald A. Luidens, *Vanishing Boundaries: The Religion of Mainline Protestant Baby Boomers* (Louisville: Westminster/John Knox, 1994).

8. For an interesting and revealing discussion of the possibility of heresy, see Thomas O. Oden and Lewis S. Mudge, "Can We Talk about Heresy?" *The Christian Century,* April 12, 1995, 390–403.

9. 2 Thessalonians 2:10.

10. Blaise Pascal, cited in Dietrich von Hildebrand, *The Charitable Anathema* (Harrison, N.Y.: Roman Catholic Books, 1993), 1.

11. David F. Wells, *No Place for Truth: Or Whatever Happened to Evangelical Theology* (Grand Rapids: Eerdmans, 1993). See also David F. Wells, *God in the Wasteland: The Reality of Truth in a World of Fading Dreams* (Grand Rapids: Eerdmans, 1994).

12. See Marsha Witten, *All Is Forgiven: The Secular Message in American Protestantism* (Princeton: Princeton University Press, 1993); and Phillip E. Hammond, *Religion and Personal Autonomy: The Third Disestablishment in America* (Columbia: University of South Carolina Press, 1992).

13. James Davison Hunter, *American Evangelicalism: Conservative Religion and the Quandry of Modernity* (New Brunswick: Rutgers University Press, 1983) and *Evangelicalism: The Coming Generation* (Chicago: University of Chicago Press, 1987).

14. See J. Richard Middleton and Brian Walsh, *Truth Is Stranger Than It Used to Be: Biblical Faith in a Postmodern Age* (Downers Grove, Ill.: InterVarsity, 1995); and Philip D. Kenneson, "There's No Such Thing as Objective Truth and It's a Good Thing, Too," in *Christian Apologetics in the Postmodern World,* ed. Timothy R. Phillips and Dennis L. Okholm (Downers Grove, Ill.: InterVarsity, 1995), 155–70. For a consideration of these issues, see R. Albert Mohler Jr., "Whither Evangelicalism? Gathering Clouds of the Present Crisis," in *The Coming Evangelical Crisis,* ed. John Armstrong (Chicago: Moody, 1996).

15. Stanley J. Grenz, *A Primer on Postmodernism* (Grand Rapids: Eerdmans, 1996), 10.

16. Stanley J. Grenz, *Revisioning Evangelical Theology: A Fresh Agenda for the 21st Century* (Downers Grove, Ill.: InterVarsity, 1993), 88.

17. The application "New Yale Theology" has become a common descriptor for a movement largely associated with the Yale Divinity School. See Mark I. Wallace, *The Second Naivete: Barth, Ricoeur, and the New Yale Theology,* Studies in American Biblical Hermeneutics 6, 2nd ed. (Macon, Ga.: Mercer University Press, 1995).

18. William H. Willimon, "Jesus' Peculiar Truth," *Christianity Today,* March 4, 1996, 21–22.

19. Ibid., 21.

20. Ibid., 22.

21. Ibid.

22. Grenz, *Revisioning*, 56–57.

23. J. Gresham Machen, "The Creeds and Doctrinal Advance," in *God Transcendent* (Edinburgh: Banner of Truth Trust), 158.

24. J. Richard Middleton and Brian J. Walsh, *Truth Is Stranger Than It Used to Be: Biblical Faith in a Postmodern Age* (Downers Grove, Ill.: InterVarsity, 1995).

25. Ibid., 178.

26. Phillip D. Kenneson, "There's No Such Thing as Objective Truth, and It's a Good Thing, Too," in *Christian Apologetics in the Postmodern World*, ed. Timothy R. Phillips and Dennis L. Okholm (Downers Grove, Ill.: InterVarsity, 1995), 155–70.

27. Ibid.

28. John Charles Ryle, *Charges and Addresses* (Edinburgh: Banner of Truth Trust, 1978 [originally published 1903]), 49–50.

29. Among contemporary evangelicals, an example of a mediating system is that offered by Stanley Grenz, who draws from George Lindbeck and others who identify the truth with a distinct "cultural linguistic system" as suggested by anthropologist Clifford Geertz. This amounts to another form of cultural relativism. See Stanley J. Grenz, *Revisioning Evangelical Theology: A Fresh Agenda for the 21st Century* (Downers Grove, Ill.: InterVarsity, 1993).

30. See Robert Brow, "The Evangelical Megashift," *Christianity Today*, February 19, 1990, 12–14. Replies from D. A. Carson, Clark H. Pinnock, Robert E. Weber, and Donald G. Bloesch follow on pp. 14–17.

31. Ryle, *Charges and Addresses*, 58.

32. Martin Luther, *TableTalk*, ed. and trans. Theodore G. Tappert, "Luther's Works," vol. 54 (Philadelphia: Fortress, 1967), 192, selection no. 32296.

33. Gordon H. Clark, *Religion, Reason, and Revelation*, 2nd ed. (Jefferson, Md.: The Trinity Foundation, 1986), 252–53.

34. R. B. Kuiper, *The Bible Tells Us So* (Edinburgh: Banner of Truth Trust, 1968).

35. Wilfred Cantwell Smith, *Religious Diversity* (New York: Harper and Row, 1976), 13.

36. From "The Chicago Statement on Biblical Inerrancy," as printed in Carl F. H. Henry, *God, Revelation and Authority*, vol. 4 (Waco: Word, 1979), 212.

37. Carl Sagan, *Cosmos* (New York: Random House, 1980), 4.

38. Romans 1:18–20.

39. Romans 1:21–24.

40. Revelation 19:11–21.

41. John Calvin, "The Necessity of Reforming the Church," in *Selected Works of John Calvin: Tracts and Letters*, vol. 1, ed. and trans. Henry Beveridge (Grand Rapids: Baker, 1983 [1844]), 233.

Chapter 4: Gene Edward Veith

1. Martin Luther, "The Large Catechism," 4. 57, in *The Book of Concord: The Confessions of the Evangelical Lutheran Church*, trans. Theodore G. Tappert (Philadelphia: Fortress, 1959), 444.

2. See H. I. Marrou, *A History of Education in Antiquity* (New York: Sheed and Ward, 1956), 334–39. I am indebted to my former student, Andrew Kern, for his research into the history of the liberal arts tradition.

3. See Douglas Wilson, *Recovering the Lost Tools of Learning* (Wheaton, Ill.: Crossway, 1991). For a good account of the conceptual and developmental basis of the *trivium*, see Dorothy L. Sayers, *The Lost Tools of Learning* (Moscow, Idaho: Canon, 1990).

4. Neil Postman, *Teaching as a Conserving Activity* (New York: Delacorte, 1979).

5. See, for example, the writings of the ex-liberal Thomas Oden, such as *Two Worlds: Notes on the Death of Modernity in America and Russia* (Downers Grove, Ill.: InterVarsity, 1992).

Chapter 5: Michael S. Horton

1. H. Richard Niebuhr, *The Kingdom of God in America* (New York: Harper and Row, 1937), 2.

2. Walter Lippmann, *A Preface to Morals* (New York: Macmillan, 1929), 3.

3. George Barna, *Marketing the Church* (Ventura, Calif.: Regal, 1992), 41, 145.

4. *Newsweek,* September 17, 1984, 26.

5. William Willimon, "Been There, Preached That," *Leadership* (Fall 1995): 75–78.

6. George Lindbeck, in *Postmodern Theology,* ed. Frederic Burnham (Harper and Row, 1989), 45.

7. Niebuhr, *Kingdom of God,* 193. Niebuhr adds, "For an Edwards divine sovereignty had been a hard truth to which he had slowly learned to adjust his thought and life; for liberalism it was an untruth. It established continuity between God and man by adjusting God to man." Consequently, "Christ the Redeemer became Jesus the teacher or the spiritual genius in whom the religious capacities of mankind were fully developed" (p. 192).

8. Eugene F. Rice, *The Foundations of Early Modern Europe* (New York: Norton, 1970), 136.

9. From Calvin's *Letter to Sadoleto,* in *Tracts and Treatises* I, 1.

10. George Barna, *What Americans Believe* (Ventura: Regal, 1991), 83–84.

11. Theodore Beza, *The Christian Faith,* trans. James Clark (East Sussex, Eng.: Focus Christian Ministries Trust, 1992), 40–41. Published first at Geneva in 1558 as the *Confession de foi du chretien.*

12. Calvin, 2.7.5 of the 1536 *Institutes,* trans. F. L. Battles (Grand Rapids: Eerdmans, 1975), 30–31; cf. 1559 *Institutes* 2.11.10.

13. Calvin, 1559 *Institutes* 3.14.13.

14. Ibid.

15. Battles edition of 1536 edition, 365. Delivered by Nicolas Cop on his assumption of the rectorship of the University of Paris; there is a wide consensus among Calvin scholars that Calvin was the author.

16. Ibid., 366.

17. Ibid., 369.

18. Ursinus, *Commentary on the Heidelberg Catechism* (Phillipsburg, N.J.: Presbyterian and Reformed, from 2nd American ed., 1852), 2.

19. Ibid., 2.

20. Charles Spurgeon, *New Park Street Pulpit,* vol. 1 (Pasadena, Tex.: Pilgrim Publications, 1975), 285.

21. Machen, *Christianity and Liberalism* (New York: Macmillan, 1923), 143.

22. Machen, *Christian Faith in the Modern World* (New York: Macmillan, 1936), 57.

23. Machen, *What Is Faith?* (New York: Macmillan, 1925), 137, 139, 152.

24. Machen, *Education, Christianity and the State* (Jefferson, Md.: The Trinity Foundation, 1987), 21.

25. Barna, *What Americans Believe,* 51.

26. Ibid., 89.

27. Ibid., 80.

28. *Newsweek,* September 17, 1984, 26–28.

29. Charles Finney, *Revivals of Religion* (Old Tappan: Revell, 1968), 2–5. Among the many contemporary examples that could be cited is the recent ad copy for the National Day of Prayer (May 2, 1996): "It's time we tapped into our most powerful natural resource." Nowhere in the copy is God viewed as the supernatural giver of all blessings in Christ; rather, prayer is a human technique that secures natural ends through natural means: "Now more than ever, our nation needs to be united. Prayer pulls us together. . . . It's essential that we use this vital resource and take the time to 'Honor God.' The returns are worth the investment. Prayer: We've always had it. It's time we used it."

30. Clark Pinnock, ed., *The Grace of God and the Will of Man* (Grand Rapids: Zondervan, 1989), 27. Further, Pinnock questions the doctrines of original sin and substitutionary atonement for reasons similar to Finney's (pp. 22–23), adding: "It is my strong impression, confirmed to me even by those not pleased by it, that Augustinian thinking is losing its hold on present-day Christians" (p. 26).

31. Charles Finney, *Systematic Theology* (Minneapolis: Bethany, 1976). On original sin, Finney takes a great deal of space attacking "the anti-scriptural and nonsensical dogma of a sinful constitution" (p. 179). Concerning the substitutionary atonement, he writes, "If he [Christ] obeyed the law as our

substitute, then why should our own return to personal obedience be insisted upon as a *sine qua non* of our salvation? . . . Example is the highest moral influence that can be exerted" (pp. 206, 209). He strongly denies the view "that the atonement was a literal payment of a debt" (p. 217). On the new birth, he insists, "Original or constitutional sinfulness, physical regeneration, and all their kindred and resulting dogmas, are alike subversive of the gospel, and repulsive to the human intelligence; and should be laid aside as relics of a most unreasonable and confused philosophy" (p. 236).

32. Finney, *Systematic Theology.* His view of justification is equally plain: "But for sinners to be forensically pronounced just, is impossible and absurd. . . . As we shall see, there are many conditions, while there is but one ground, of the justification of sinners. . . . As has been already said, there can be no justification in a legal or forensic sense, but upon the ground of universal, perfect, and uninterrupted obedience to law. . . . The doctrine of an imputed righteousness, or that Christ's obedience to the law was accounted as our obedience, is founded on a most false and nonsensical assumption," that assumption being the substitutionary atonement (pp. 320–21).

33. Russell Spittler, in *Christian Spirituality: Five Views of Sanctification,* ed. Donald L. Alexander (Downers Grove, Ill.: InterVarsity, 1988), 43.

34. Clark Pinnock, in *Four Views of Hell* (Grand Rapids: Zondervan, 1992), 122–31.

35. Stanley Grenz, in *Revisioning Evangelical Theology* (IVP, 1993), argues for a definition of evangelical in terms of shared experiences, stories, and piety rather than in terms of doctrine. Kenneth Kantzer endorses it as a volume that "redefines evangelicalism as focusing, not on its doctrinal commitments, but on a type of spiritual experience or piety. In so doing he says many things that ought to be heard and heeded by all Christians." Critical of "Reformation confessionalism," Grenz appeals to the pietistic side of the evangelical heritage, but one might conclude

from the almost exclusive priority given to narrative and existential categories that this is a euphemism for theological relativism. Other examples of "new-model" literature include the contributors (Richard Rice, John Sanders, William Hasker, David Basinger) to *The Openness of God* (IVP, 1994); Robert Brow, author of the *Christianity Today* article on the "megashift" (February 19, 1990) and co-author with Pinnock of *Unbounded Love* (IVP, 1994). The question as to whether both pietism and Arminianism are being used as terms for legitimizing within evangelicalism something that actually is more radical than both of these movements is brought into focus also in reading *The Grace of God and the Will of Man: A Case for Arminianism* (Zondervan, 1989), edited by Pinnock with contributors such as respected New Testament scholar I. Howard Marshall, Terry Miethe, and Grant Osborne. A symposium on the "megashift," with Clark Pinnock, Robert Webber, and Richard Rice defending the "new model" against representatives of the so-called "old model" is available from Christians United for Reformation (CURE), Anaheim, California.

36. Ray S. Anderson, *The Gospel According to Judas* (Colorado Springs: Helmer and Howard, 1991), 99.

37. *Newsweek,* August 9, 1993.

Chapter 6: Sinclair B. Ferguson

1. Roland Bainton, *Here I Stand* (Abingdon: Nashville, 1978 [1950]), 67.

2. *The Confession of Faith* (1647), chap. XV.iii.

3. W. L. Holladay, *The Root Sub in the Old Testament: With Particular Reference to Its Usages in Covenantal Contexts* (Leiden: E. J. Brill, 1958), 1, 116–55.

4. Cited in Bainton, *Here I Stand,* 48.

5. See chapter title of *Institutes,* III.iii.1.

6. John Calvin, *Commentary on the Acts of the Apostles, 14–28,* trans. J. W. Fraser, ed. D. W. and T. F. Torrance (Edinburgh, 1966), 176.

7. *Institutes,* III.iii. 3.

8. John Calvin, *The Epistle of Paul the Apostle to the Hebrews; The Epistles of Peter,* trans. W. B. Johnstone, ed. D. W. and T. F. Torrance (Edinburgh, 1963), 240.

9. John Calvin, *The Epistles of Paul the Apostle to the Romans and to the Thessalonians,* trans. Ross Mackenzie, ed. D. W. and T. F. Torrance (Edinburgh, 1960), 167.

10. *Canons and Decrees of the Council of Trent,* On the Sacraments in General, Canon IX.

11. *The Confession of Faith,* XV.i, ii.

12. *The Confession of Faith,* I.vii.

13. Thomas McCrie, *The Story of the Scottish Church* (London, 1875), 248.

14. *The Confession of Faith,* XV.v.

15. Drawn up in 1651, this confession is accessible in: Horatius Bonar, *Words to Winners of Souls* (Boston, 1860; Phillipsburg, N.J.: Presbyterian and Reformed and the den Dulk Foundation, 1995 reprint), 25–34.

Chapter 7: W. Robert Godfrey

1. Augustine, *Confessions,* Books 7–9.

2. "Smalcald Articles," Article 2, cited from T. G. Tappert, ed., *The Book of Confessions* (Philadelphia: Fortress, 1959), 293.

3. Martin Luther, *Luther's Works,* vol. 54 (Philadelphia: Fortress, 1967), 340.

4. John Calvin, "Reply to Sadoleto," in *A Reformation Debate,* ed. John C. Olin (New York: Harper, 1966), 63.

5. Ibid., 87.

6. John Calvin, "The Necessity of Reforming the Church," in *Selected Works of John Calvin,* ed. Henry Beveridge and Jules Bonnet, vol. 1 (Grand Rapids: Baker, 1983), 125.

7. See, for example, Nathan Hatch, *The Democratization of American Christianity* (New Haven: Yale University Press, 1989).

8. William T. Ellis, *"Billy" Sunday,* 1914, 264.

9. D. G. Hart, "Post-Modern Evangelical Worship," *Calvin Theological Journal* 30 (1995): 454.

10. Robert Webber, *Signs of Wonder: The Phenomenon of Convergence in Modern Liturgical and Charismatic Churches* (Nashville: Abbott-Martyn, 1992).

11. Charles G. Finney, *Revivals of Religion* (Old Tappan, N.J.: Revell, n.d.), 2.

12. Ibid., 4.

13. Cited in Keith Hardman, *Charles Grandison Finney, 1792–1875* (Syracuse, N.Y.: Syracuse University Press), 199.

14. See, for example, Larry B. Stammer, "Church Attendance Falls to 11-Year Low," *Los Angeles Times,* March 2, 1996, pp. B4f. This article, based on the surveying of the Barna Research Group Ltd., shows that in the past five years church attendance in America has declined from 49 percent to 37 percent.

15. See the surveys discussed in James Davison Hunter, *Evangelicalism: The Coming Generation* (Chicago: University of Chicago Press, 1987); and David Wells, *God in the Wasteland: The Reality of Truth in a World of Fading Dreams* (Grand Rapids: Eerdmans, 1994).

16. John Calvin, "The True Method of Giving Peace to Christendom and Reforming the Church," in *Selected Works of John Calvin,* vol. 3, 260.

17. Calvin, "Reply to Sadoleto," 58.

18. Hunter, *Evangelicalism,* 183.

19. Calvin, "Reply to Sadoleto," 53.

20. Calvin, "True Method," 274.

21. See, for example, Clark Pinnock et al., *The Openness of God* (Downers Grove, Ill.: InterVarsity, 1994); and Clark Pinnock and Robert Brow, *Unbounded Love* (Downers Grove, Ill.: InterVarsity, 1994).

22. See, for example, Virginia Mollenkott, *Sensuous Spirituality* (New York: Crossroad, 1992); and Hessel Bouma III et al., *Christian Faith, Health, and Medical Practice* (Grand Rapids: Eerdmans, 1989).

23. B. B. Warfield, *Perfectionism,* vol. 2 (New York: Oxford University Press, 1931), 193, cited by Hardman, *Finney,* 394.

24. Calvin, "True Method," 295.

Chapter 8: James M. Boice

1. David F. Wells, *God in the Wasteland: The Reality of Truth in a World of Fading Dreams* (Grand Rapids: Eerdmans, and Leicester, England: InterVarsity, 1994), 30.

2. Ibid., 115.

3. Arthur W. Pink, *The Sovereignty of God* (Grand Rapids: Baker, 1969), 263.

4. Emil Brunner, *The Christian Doctrine of God,* trans. Olive Wyon, vol. 1 (Philadelphia: Westminster, 1950), 157.

5. Wells, *God in the Wasteland,* 133.

6. Karl Menninger, *Whatever Became of Sin?* (New York: Bantam, 1978).

7. Ibid., flyleaf.

8. Wells, *God in the Wasteland,* 136.

9. Charles Hodge, *Systematic Theology,* vol. 1 (London: James Clarke, 1960), 401.

10. J. I. Packer, *Knowing God* (Downers Grove, Ill.: InterVarsity, 1973), 80–81.

11. Martin Luther, *What Luther Says: An Anthology,* comp. Ewald M. Plass, vol. 3 (St. Louis: Concordia, 1959), 1453.

12. John R. W. Stott, *Christ the Controversialist: A Study in Some Essentials of Evangelical Religion* (London: Tyndale, 1970), 160.

13. A. W. Tozer, *The Pursuit of God* (Harrisburg, Pa.: Christian Publications, 1948), 9.

14. William Temple, *The Hope of a New World,* 30. Cited by Donald P. Hustad, *Jubilate! Church Music in the Evangelical Tradition* (Carol Stream, Ill.: Hope, 1981), 78.

15. R. Kent Hughes, *Disciplines of a Godly Man* (Wheaton, Ill.: Crossway, 1991), 106.

16. William Barclay, *The Gospel of John,* vol. 1 (Philadelphia: Westminster, 1958), 154.

17. C. S. Lewis, *Letters to Malcolm: Chiefly on Prayer* (New York: Harcourt, Brace, and World, 1963), 4.

18. Augustine, *The City of God,* in *A Select Library of the Nicene and Post-Nicene Fathers of the Christian Church,* ed. Philip Schaff, vol. 2 (Grand Rapids: Eerdmans, 1977), 282–83.

19. Anthony T. Evans, "10 Steps to Urban Renewal," *The Urban Alternative* 4, no. 2 (September 1988).

20. Charles Reich, *The Greening of America: The Coming of a New Consciousness and the Rebirth of a Future* (New York: Bantam, 1971), 7.

21. Michael Scott Horton, *Made in America: The Shaping of Modern American Evangelicalism* (Grand Rapids: Baker, 1991), 169.

Index

James Montgomery Boice is senior pastor of Philadelphia's historic Tenth Presbyterian Church and the speaker on "The Bible Study Hour," a radio program broadcast nationally. He is the author or editor of nearly forty books, including *Foundations of the Christian Faith* and *Standing on the Rock: Biblical Authority in a Secular Age.*

Benjamin E. Sasse is executive director of the Alliance of Confessing Evangelicals (ACE) and of Christians United for Reformation (CURE). He earned an A.B. in government from Harvard University, and he has worked for the Boston Consulting Group, a strategy management consulting firm. This is his first book.